AF611451

# The Laws of Nature for Better Business

Order this book online at www.trafford.com/08-0440
or email orders@trafford.com

Most Trafford titles are also available at major online book retailers.



Cover Design/Artwork by Real Brand and Business
Design by Chris Walker
Layout and Content design by Helena Rodriguez Walker
Edited by Helena Rodriguez Walker

Note for Librarians: A cataloguing record for this book is available from Library and Archives Canada at www.collectionscanada.ca/amicus/index-e.html

ISBN: 978-1-4251-7534-4

*We at Trafford believe that it is the responsibility of us all, as both individuals and corporations, to make choices that are environmentally and socially sound. You, in turn, are supporting this responsible conduct each time you purchase a Trafford book, or make use of our publishing services. To find out how you are helping, please visit www.trafford.com/responsiblepublishing.html*

*Our mission is to efficiently provide the world's finest, most comprehensive book publishing service, enabling every author to experience success. To find out how to publish your book, your way, and have it available worldwide, visit us online at www.trafford.com/10510*

www.trafford.com

**North America & international**
toll-free: 1 888 232 4444 (USA & Canada)
phone: 250 383 6864 • fax: 250 383 6804 • email: info@trafford.com

**The United Kingdom & Europe**
phone: +44 (0)1865 487 395 • local rate: 0845 230 9601
facsimile: +44 (0)1865 481 507 • email: info.uk@trafford.com

10 9 8 7 6 5 4 3

We consider our environment, we print on post-consumer recycled paper

There are great masters such as Emerson, Plato and many Asian Masters (Lao Tzu) who are convinced that if mankind lived life according to the principles of Nature, then we would be at peace with ourselves and with each other. It's a philosophy not uncommon in the ways of the East but has yet to be fully grasped by the western world. We are hoping this modern way of presenting this ancient theme will resonate with you, irrespective of your cultural or religious background.

## Dedication

Thank you to all the wonderful people who helped me put this book together. To Helena, Virginia, Kim, Tasha, Simon, Adam, David, and to the nearly 3500 clients who have put their trust in me for guidance over these past 10 years. Thank you for allowing me to use the ghosts of those stories here. Also, thanks to my First Nation Friends in Canada where the Laws of Nature and the spirit of real life came hand to hand. To all those beautiful people who have supported this mission to bring a better humanity to business and life. Thank you from the depths of my heart.

Chris Walker

Sydney - Australia September 1, 2008

G'Day from Chris Walker,

The Laws of Nature manage the Universe, so, they have a pretty good possibility of helping you manage your organisation and your own work life.

This book takes the fastest, simplest and most profound Personal Growth Process on earth, and applies it to organisational leadership, management, self-management and work life balance.

We need it. We need a fresh approach to management. One that's not based on the arts of war or reactive ideology but a proactive, socially responsible, personally inspiring way to work, that actually builds great family lives, rather than challenge them.

We begin the book talking about being FIT. This word is often applied to our state of personal health, but it is incredibly important for our organisations too. From one person business to whole nations, being FIT means that where we're going, what we need to go there and the human capacity to do it are all working hand in hand. All too often they are not and the consequences of that need no explanation.

Harmony only comes when all the elements FIT together and work together. I think you'll find that 90% of personal stress comes as a result of bad management - poor FIT. This book aims to bring Nature to the boardroom just as my other books bought Nature to the bedroom to help people live in harmony without compromising their intent.

We've also included a Culture Audit that you can do yourself and then a great process for determining the GAP between where your organisation is today, and where it needs to be, in Human Resources terms, for the future.

Now, you'll know where you are and where you need to be. The rest of the book shares how to get there, hand in hand with the most powerful tools of Personal Growth, all taken from the realms of Nature.

I hope you love it as much as I have by spending the last 20 years of my life preparing and researching for it. I hope it grabs you in your heart and inspires you. In Australia we say G'day, it means, "Have a Great Day," and this book is designed to help you do just that, no matter what your job.

# Contents

# Introduction

Since Nature is the keeper of sacred law, it is a worthy beginning to ask her to share principles of reality. The forest, the ocean, the sky, species, plants; animal's insects have a voice. It will require the deepest silence to hear it.

## The Laws of Nature

The order of things is magnificent. The key to that perfect order is available. The more order, the more beauty you see - the more of this beauty you see the more empowered - inspired - motivated you become. With this expansion, you write more songs, dance with more vitality, paint more paintings, sell more cars, feed more children, make more bread, and give more to others.

It's Nature's equation. The more of the perfect order you can see the more you are inspired by life itself. It's a cycle, see more beauty, be inspired by life, and seek more beauty. When you see a great leader in any field, they are usually a person who can see great things, vision great things. Some people are born with that seeing, some people are born with none. However, everyone has access to it.

It won't come from books, workshops, coaching, money, or success. It comes from you and the choices you make. Nature is the mirror of the perfect order so she is the perfect teacher. To learn, you simply look inside your own heart and ask what do you love doing. What are you inspired about? You have to get to the point that what you are inspired about is incorporated into the whole of your life. Linking what you love to what you do is the real Nature of humanity, living inspired. This is a great gift to others too, because instead of dragging others down, or around, you become an inspiration to people by being inspired.

The Laws of Nature are more commonly referred to as, "the Universal Laws." They are a profound insight into the source, cause and awareness of life. If you were to ask, "what was God thinking when he or she created the universe, the Universal Laws, are it.

These laws repeat themselves everywhere, all the way down to the smallest of smallest particle of human existence right here on earth.

What an amazing thought! A set of non-emotional, non-judgemental principles that can explain creation, and for that matter, destruction. Even in your business, your happiness, your health and your relationship. It's an unbelievable insight into how, when, where and why things happen the way they do.

The world has changed. Things go faster, communication is easier. Technological advantage is only a week in advance of the copycat. Satellites watch us, the stock market pre-empts our decisions. Good practice is becoming more the norm, and we are struggling to keep up at a human level.

All the world evolves, specie die, things become extinct, business go bad, new ones start but those organisations, business and people that evolve, don't go bad, they sustain themselves in a healthy state. And those employees that evolve sustain employment. Those individuals that evolve in harmony with Nature stay healthy, and those relationships that evolve, stay together. Evolution is the key to sustainability. The ability to grow, in the right direction, is a powerful asset for everyone in all walks of life.

The Universal Laws are a vital and important awareness in helping a re emergence of a unified humanity on earth. We need to find the sticking points where old belief patterns and old paradigms of human management are still stuck, in particular in Business Management.

The universal Laws of Nature explain things from a universal perspective. That's a pretty big perspective, don't you agree? When I apply them to everyday life, then everything is ordered, I find contentment. This is far beyond the ideas of faith or trust. These laws explain with absolute predictability the dynamics of life.

Even when I was in New York, and the World Trade Center was attacked I was able to hold my heart in a good place because I understood the universal Laws of Nature. One part of me screamed in agony, my ego - emotional body - was in shock, but my heart and mind were calm because I could understand the reality of the situation from a higher perspective.

This was a defining moment in my life because even in the most extreme circumstance I could remain connected to the earth; I could hold my own commitment to helping others. By applying the Laws of Nature, the universal law, I could hold a non-reactive space and help others.

On that day, I felt such love, and I felt such pain. One part of me was grounded in holding the order in the chaos, while my emotions wanted to scream in agony at the trauma. I think this is an extreme example and it may feel offensive to some of the victims of that disaster. Please don't think I am diminishing the suffering because this is not my intent. I just want to explain that we now have a tool to hold us stable in our deepest soul, while we face all manner of challenge in life.

In the next pages are the Laws of Nature. Be proud that you are reading such ancient knowledge and remember that it's not just for your own benefit that you take the time to explore them. Treasure the amazing awareness they will give you.

When the spirit of nature comes into your heart, you feel connected to great wisdom. Nothing much can shift you off your track when you get this gift and once you've got it, you can't lose it.

This book brings the spirit of nature into the workplace.

You can feel it when an organisation has this energy. It's a buzz and it shows in people's faces and the bottom line of the company. Clients know it too.

Once, this connection was natural, we worked with our hands and we knew the basics of life. But we lost it and I hope this book and the seminars that follow it can help to keep us all connected to the earth, and the spirit of nature.

## Universal Law 1 - Balance

There are two sides to everything. All emotion is a lie. Judgements see one side of a two-sided coin. Reaction and rejection all come from the human mind trying to live out of harmony with Nature. Social chaos, ill health, mental exhaustion, war, violence and addiction all lead back to a disharmony with Nature's law of balance. There are two sides to everything. We can't even manage a business if we can't see the balance in it. The person, who can see balance in circumstance, rises out of judgement and fear. They are the ones who make great decisions, birth creativity, inspire others, create great art and think from their genius. Every human is capable of this but only with balanced thought.

## Universal Law 2 - Evolution

All things evolve. Nature destroys those things that don't evolve. It's a process of continuous improvement. When we stop learning, we die. When a business stops refining it's process, it also dies. Many circumstances in life are explained by this one principle of Nature. Relationships, for example, that don't grow, end up miserable. Every tree, bush, animal, river, ocean is evolving. Continuously improving toward a destiny. From ashes to ashes, dust-to-dust, we are returning from whence we came. From Star stuff we came, to star stuff we go. We are on an evolving planet, in an evolving universe. We either evolve or get off the bus. It is the greatest recycling system imaginable. Matter that doesn't fulfil its purpose gets recycled. Harmony with Nature means, simply, evolving in step with the universe. Ill health is one of the most aggressive awareness that we are out of step with evolution. The key here is the process of building the new on top of the old, greater in consciousness, less in number. In other words, those things that don't evolve, get left in the dust their matter recycled. This is history.

## Universal Law 3 - Interconnectedness

We are one world only separated by egos. All our judgements are self-judgement. The world is just one great mirror. There is nothing outside of us, that can't be found within. Spirit and matter are separated by the ego, but are inseparable to the soul. We are greater than we think, we are less important than we think. We are part of a soup, a massive soup in which energy flows and in which everything is impermanent, nothing stays fixed, yet, it's a closed loop, nothing added nothing subtracted, only changed in form. Nothing is permanent. Nothing lasts for more than a few hundred years. Yet, the essence of everything, past and future is here in the moment. We are never separated, what we do to others we do to ourselves. Our ego is such a small idea of identity. We are everything, yet, because we are part of the soup, we are nothing. As above - So below. We are spirit and we are matter, really, we are everything and everything is a part of us. What we judge in others is really ourselves. Although we divide the world into things, and separate ourselves into individuals using our beliefs and egos, we are all made of the same stuff. Break a rock and its finite particles are made of the same stuff as a human kiss. We are everything, and everything is a part of us, even if, through our limited senses, it doesn't seem like this at first. This is the real meaning of abundance. There is nothing to attract. We already have it.

## Universal Law 4 - Harmony

The whole universe is a symphony of vibrations. The heaviest object has no energy invested in spirit (vibration) and 100% invested in matter. This is a black hole. All energy has gone from spirit to matter. The lightest object is light itself; it has no energy invested in matter it is weightless, charge-less, all the energy is invested in vibration. This is the source of enlightenment – No matter – only pure light - love. Everything else, is somewhere between these two extremes. Our thoughts can change this equation from vibration to matter and from matter to vibration. We can think and change the vibration of atoms, molecules and sub atomic particles. Human beings can, on a microscopic level change vibration to matter and matter to vibration at a very microscopic level. So, we can change the form of energy. We can with the power of thought, change the form of what we already have. The law of harmony is the law of mind; we can shift energy purely through thought. The darkest thought is an ungrateful thought; (I don't have what I want) the lightest thought is a grateful thought (I already have what I want there is nothing I need to attract, I already have it). Ungrateful thoughts produce illness, breakdown, destruction, violence, self-abuse and addiction. Grateful thoughts bring love, peace of mind, happiness and joy.

Everything vibrates and at the most microscopic level human thought can change those vibrations. We can cause harmony, and we can cause disharmony. Thoughts can change the world. Harmony builds, disharmony shrinks.

### Universal Law 5. The One and the Many

You may ask; what direction is evolution? You may ask; why do we have egos and emotions that contradict the law of balance? You may ask; why do we not know that we are all one world? You may also question; why do only a few people know the secrets of manifestation with thought? The answer is here, the fifth law of the Universe. All the parts report to the whole. The lower elements of life all report to the upper elements. Then, those upper elements report to higher elements. The many report to the one. Everything is humble to a greater organizing force. Ants report to a higher order, otherwise there would be chaos. Lions in the jungle have a governing law that evolves them, the survival of the fittest. A company has a CEO or a board. A beehive has a queen. There is an organizing force that causes all existence to conform to a higher law. Everything looks free, but isn't. We are, in fact, on a journey even though we think we have free will and can live or die, we are part of a far greater plan. Our business, our health and our relationships are microcosms in which we think we are independent, but these too, like the ants or the lions, are controlled by far greater principles than human emotions. We report to the universe, and the universe to... nothing, absolutely nothing is random and the one who learns this is truly a lucky soul, no matter what the circumstance of their apparent material life.

# Chapter 1.
# Is Your Organisation FIT?

Any organisation is only as good as its people and its people are only as good as the speed with which they adapt to change.

# The New Organisation

The greatest asset any organisation can have is the ability to adapt to change. That ability is really 100% human. Everything in the universe changes, including your organisation but the human factor in this has been dragging the anchor for too long. To change your organisation's strategy takes a weekend and to change your organisation's resources or structure, takes a month at the most but when it comes to changing your organisation's culture, human behaviour, well, we may as well take a cut lunch and go on holiday while it happens. It has traditionally taken years. And we no longer have that luxury.

The human cost of change has been huge. When people don't adapt to the changing environment in business, they get stressed, blow out their home life, or have a personal crash. The cost is massive because many of these broken individuals stay employed within that organisation. Not only is the human cost too high, but also the capacity for organisations to "carry" the wounded, people who couldn't keep up with change, has gone.

Rather than deal with the problems that come from the human fallout from this new and rapid demand for adaptability in business, the human breakdowns, I think we need to deal with the cause. I've owned Yoga schools and worked in health retreats for burned out executives, I healed the broken families and experienced these things first hand. People, who don't learn to adapt to change, really pay the highest price of all. And I believe, it is totally unnecessary.

I am going to introduce a new word to you at this stage. It's not a new word in language but it might be a new word in your management philosophy. That word is 'evolve'. Evolve means harmony with change, it means the ability to be proactive in change, it means that people adapt daily, not every 7 years with divorces, health farms or addiction clinics. Evolve means to adapt and the people who are going to suffer from the incorporation of this word in organisational management are the medical profession, drug companies and healers who thrive on corporate fallout.

Let's put a stop to the human breakdowns that come from bad management practice. If you are ready, it begins here, with you.

# FIT for Work

There are three ingredients of organisational change that must FIT together. If they don't, change doesn't happen or more accurately, change happens at a huge human cost.

Great, painless, fast organisational change requires that three core ingredients of any entity FIT together. These three are:

Strategy - The direction the organisation wants to travel toward.

Structure - The resources, systems, human and material to go there.

Culture - The right behaviour to cause it happen.

When those three are in FIT you can safely say, the organisation is Evolving forward. People are on board, strategy is clear and the resources are adapting to the demands of the new environment.

Too many organisations get two out of three right, and then go bust or don't support the individuals within them. You can see how easy it is to sit in a think tank, create a vision, love your team and think: "they'll grow into it." This is really UNFIT management. The human cost of organisations that are out of harmony with their strategy going one way, their resources being assembled in another and their culture off on a tangent lingering in the past somewhere is huge. My motto is that hard work is bad management and I mean it. When an organisation is in FIT, between its strategy, structure and culture, the market knows it, the people inside the organisation know it, and the stakeholders know it.

It is the new core responsibility of a manager to get this right. Even at a departmental level there are sub-strategies, sub-cultures and sub-structures. These need to FIT and if they don't then disharmony happens.

The net result of disharmony is stress, unproductive time, profit decline, market rejection and internal turmoil way above healthy levels. Then, if there's a disharmony, UNFIT Management, even the best training, conference, leader, pay rise, motivational speech, will fail.

# Disharmony Is Infectious

Three ways For Organisational Change – Two hurt – One Doesn't.

The fastest and most painful way to change a culture is with a big chequebook. One entrepreneur who buys and sells a multi national business, sets down his strategy for change within the organisation. Fire half the staff and pay the rest double.

The second fastest way to change a culture is shock: this is in the form of a massive overhaul such as a take-over, a reorganisation or a complete change in ownership. Those shocks usually come in the form of a market crash, a business failure or bankruptcy. This is also a fast and very painful way of causing change.

99% of the reason that the first two painful methods of organisational change have to happen is because people don't evolve their work practices. Ultimately, people reach their level of incompetence in an organisation and then the whole machine stalls. Even one person can be responsible for stalling growth in a culture involving hundreds of people if their methods are loud and righteous.

Ultimately people pay a high price for their inability to adapt to change in these first two models where resistance is futile and shock or force is used to cause growth. But the cost has already been far higher than we think. People who can't adapt to the changing environment and who resist, have the most domestic trouble, the greatest ill health, the most stress. They have it because they bring the disharmony home in their heart, mind and body. The cost rolls out into families, children and society. Doctors prescribe drugs, pharmacies dispense remedies, but no pill can mend a broken heart. The costs to everyone are huge.

When people don't have the willingness or intent to adapt to change they become, in the evolution of an organisation, the equivalent to dead wood on a tree. So, the model of holding onto employees long term doesn't apply anymore. If a person doesn't adapt, Nature itself will bring in the tsunami and move them. This is called: a takeover, a retrenchment, downsizing, sick leave, divorce, stress or nervous breakdown. The bottom line: People who can't evolve get sick or fired.

# 3rd Method of Organisational Change

In Nature, everything is adapting. Buckminster Fuller said, "There's no such thing as pollution, there's just environments we haven't got used to yet." It's a bit tough but what he was referring to was the essential capacity of Nature and humans to adapt to change. To go with the flow.

Many scientists say that 90% of the specie on earth, plants and animals are extinct but they are totally misguided. Nature never destroys anything; she simply builds a new one on top of the old one, greater in consciousness, less in number. The point being that inside an elephant there would be the DNA of a Dinosaur. (It doesn't take much to see that inside many violent humans, the DNA of primitive cave people still exists.)

Organisations adapt too. Whereas, the Dinosaur might evolve because of the environment or human threat, organisations adapt because if they don't they go bust. If you are searching for the reason any organisation failed to make enough profit, look no further than the capacity of the people within it to adapt, evolve to meet the demands of the world it serves.

The third, and most non-violent method of change is called evolution. It means that there is a single-minded goal of every person working within that organisation to improve the process, and that simply means: get more done in less time without quality failure. In this new paradigm everyone becomes a change agent. And where do they look for growth?

They look at themselves. The key to a fast adapting, market savvy organisation in any industry and of any size is the capacity of the individuals within the organisation to evolve. This means a focus on own time management, process, productivity, personal wellness and, most importantly, the ability to learn from challenge.

Nature has always used challenge to stimulate change. In fact, maximum sustainable growth of any organisation, human, Nature, animal or business, is at the border of order (all going peacefully) and chaos, (all gone to hell in a handbag).

# The Middle Path

There is no stimulation for growth on the middle path because there doesn't need to be. If we evolve daily, we're fluctuating between order and chaos in small bites. However, if we're addicted to peace and we define a great working day as the avoidance of challenge, then we're going to have a nice long comfortable period of peace and goodwill to all human beings, followed by a period of total disaster.

Just go out the front door and into Nature and observe how the universe works. Don't take my word for it. Observe countries or tribes that stay relatively isolated and untouched by challenge from the outside, and then see what happens. War or disease or a Tsunami.

Nothing escapes the parameters of support and challenge. It's called Love. Yeah, I know it's a business book, but this is such a cool awareness. Love is the balance between support and challenge and everything in the universe grows along the border of support and challenge so, everything is loved. Nice huh?

The corporate issue is that many people can structure their roles in corporations to avoid detection by the challenge aspect of Nature. They might own the company, they might be making profits and all seems fantastic, until a health scare, a family breakdown or the business runs out of cash. This individual has been hiding from reality.

Everything, everyone, no matter who, where, why or what they do, evolves at the border of chaos and order. So, even the peace people have balance of chaos. Even the Dali Lama will say that Tibet got invaded because it got stuck in isolation, it attracted the chaos because it closed it's borders.

Now, we come back to people, change, evolution and growth of organisations. When people resist change, when they hold onto their safety and don't adapt to the demands of their customers they hold total organisations from smooth evolution. When support and challenge become chunky, there's a honeymoon and then there's a takeover or an internal tsunami. The ability for organisations to implement their cleverly thought out strategy comes down to the ability of its people to adapt, evolve and grow continuously from challenge.

# Holistic Thinking - Real balance

We've established that organisations evolve along the border of chaos and order. We've noted that the fluctuations between chaos and order can be small daily and personal or they can be huge, annually and organisational.

However, there is another side to this equation that is worthy of your consideration. This topic drives to the heart of compassionate leadership and flips over many of the classical paradigms of good employment policy. And this is it.

If a person does not evolve their work practices, they can remain in "order" for an extended period of time, unchallenged at work and if Nature is always seeking to balance chaos with order, support with challenge (there's that love word again in a business book) well, the question might be, "where is the challenge for a person who is resisting adaptation in their work life?" The answer is, "at home."

The increased pressure on relationships to survive, and for people to stay immune from bugs, virus, and disease can be one of the most measurable consequences of resistance to change at work that we have. If people are not adapting in their work practices, management style, work process, then their challenge balance is going to come from home.

Compassion at work has classically been to be kind to people, to keep them employed, to help them stay immune from challenges to their paradigms of life. Yet, there's a point where this can become quite cruel. If we hold people in an organisation when they resist growth, when they refuse to adapt, when they are hell bent on creating a comfort zone for their work life, we're actually screwing with their home life.

It's a consideration that came home to me in a consulting brief I was offered but refused to accept in Canada. The CEO had a passion for spirituality at work, peaceful meditation and had absolute statistics to prove her achievement had reduced work stress, helped people be more relaxed and improved productivity. But she refused to measure where the challenge had gone. No body had evolved their work practice, they'd just created comfort: and sent the challenge home.

# Proactive Change - Evolve

Challenge happens in large doses when we have had periods of complacency. This means that, even if we have taken courses and studied ourselves at yoga, if we get a huge challenge, we've been doing comfort, not growth.

When an organisation faces rapid downsizing, or reengineering it means that the management has been incompetent. That incompetence has not been deliberate so, there's no need to be angry with them, or yourself. It just means they took their eye off the ball and became unconscious. Of course Nature doesn't leave anything in that state for long, so, rapid change is the tsunami we need, not the one we want.

When organisations or the people in them don't evolve (we've called this, "culture change") then there's really only one end result and that is big change, fast. We've already seen that big change fast is usually associated with significant human suffering. People losing jobs and having their private life threatened. So, I think there is a massive incentive to bring proactive change, evolution to organisational management.

The single most important thing about this is to acknowledge that large challenge reveals that there's been an extended period of bad management leading up to that need. Now, sometimes we can get confused because what we are calling bad management here, is often what managers call, good management.

Bad management in our definition comes when people don't push their staff to improve their productivity. Bad management in our definition is when people get left to their own resources, and feel empowered to make choices. Bad management in this definition is when management gives people a chance to control their environment. Bad management is listening to complaints that blame the company for stress.

Good management both supports and challenges people. (There's that L word again) - People who aren't challenged, or who learn skills at avoiding challenge, or who respond to challenge violently, are not evolving. So, good management means supporting and challenging.

# Fast Culture Change - Self-management

The real shift in organisational management is that the power to trigger growth must be placed firmly and squarely in the hands of individuals. Management is going to be too clumsy, too lumpy to evolve culture fast. So each and every individual in a fast changing culture must be skilled and willing to evolve. Management then has the role to monitor, coach and support (and challenge) the individual process.

The key ingredient of good evolving management practice is the setting of cultural and structural standards. Boundaries. When expectations are clear people can be given the skills to be creative in their self-management. So often management fails in this regard. They free the boundaries of work and therefore don't communicate the vital information that will trigger growth. Take time management for example:

If you give a person a week to do a job, how long do you think they'll take? Yes, that's it. A week and sometimes a few more days. If the bus is coming at 9.00am most people rush to catch it on time. If the bus schedule changes to 9.30am after 2 weeks they'll be rushing to catch that too. Work expands to fill the time we give it.

To evolve our work practices there are just two variables we need to focus on. They are: What we do and how long it takes. The key to evolving is to increase the quality of what we do, and do it faster. So, in an evolving organisation, one that isn't going to have a huge calamity to deal with at the end of a year, we're going to need a constant reminder, do it better and do it in less time thus do more.

You'll be surprised at how many people resist this notion. People really do resist change. The most resistant are the ones who refuse to change anything except to create more comfort for themselves. This is devolution and in a sudden organisational reshuffle, if laws allow free market behaviour, these are the first out the door.

This book shares ways to evolve yourself at work. They carry home too, because if we get stuck resisting change at home, there's going to be chaos there too. Think it through, "the pain of regret outweighs the pain of discipline."

# Clear Expectations for the Future

FIT organisations set cultural norms for the future. They ask, "What culture will we need in a few years from now in order to implement that strategy?" This culture reflects the attitudes, aptitudes and core self-management skills people will need.

It requires adaptability. Each and every individual can either grow their self-management practice and stay valuable to the organisation or they can resist and find another less demanding environment to work.

I know this sounds harsh, but how can a healthy tree hold onto dead leaves, how can a forest remain healthy if the dead wood is not cleared. Mobility in employment is a thing of the future. Organisations are going to recognise that there are varying degrees of consciousness at work and some people really don't want to evolve their ways. It might be too invasive. Then the kindest and most compassionate way to treat people, who don't evolve into the future, is to outplace them. I think this is called, "you're fired," in the USA.

The upside down model of organisational management is when people don't want, or like to evolve their ways. They've been managing the same way for years and the increased stress is causing them to reduce their workload, take more time off and go on more health programs. This is when the culture runs the company, and it is doomed to cause a major disaster.

When management fails to challenge individuals, set standards for personal growth and clear expectations; then they are placing values-based leadership over the top of growth, or humanitarian values over the top of strategic ones. There may be some government-funded organisations that can thrive under this paradigm for a while, but no competitive, market focussed organisation can.

If people don't evolve, the inevitable result is change, harsh, aggressive, fast and heartless change. There is no option; it's either a daily shake or an annual earthquake.

# A Healthy, Evolving Organisation - FIT

What does a healthy, evolving organisation look like?

1. It has a FIT boss.

Forget the rest if the boss is confused, desperate, in panic or stressed. If the boss is emotionally disturbed, emotionally ambitious or over worked, then, they are not the boss. A boss knows where their organisation or department is headed, they know why and they certainly know how and when. The boss, in whatever way they choose, sets the strategy and they'd better believe in it, and know how to achieve it, no excuses.

2. It has well managed resources.

Desperation breeds desperate people. Desperate people don't grow, evolve or change their process unless they have to. So, resource management is essential for a good boss to implement their strategy. If the boss can't manage resource, they'll not be able to implement their strategy. They go hand in hand.

3. It has a plan for people growth.

The skills a person has today are out dated tomorrow if they don't evolve them. So, a year from today, if there's not a significant growth in people skill and if it weren't for the experience factor, organisations would simply change their staff and update with people who are "current" with demands. Of course, experience is a vital factor, but not like before. So, in an evolving, healthy organisation, people enjoy challenge, learn from mistakes, explore options.

4. It has open-minded communications.

The most important human skill in a healthy, evolving organisation is the ability to enjoy diversity. That's an open-minded approach to ideas, a willingness to see balance, an understanding of emotional stability and a keen eye for self-righteous egoism, that unconscious gene that kills growth and stifles evolution.

# Healthy, Evolving People - FIT for Work

Given that an organisation can only grow as fast as its people, and that culture change is a vital part of implementing strategy, it seems obvious that helping people grow, might just be the most important human resource function there is.

Before we step into this realm, there's a warning. Some people don't want to change. And, it is completely invasive to ask people who are stuck in their ways to change them. Because of that, remember the old quote, "if you can't fire them, don't hire them." Especially with family, relatives and friends. I've witnessed more organisational suffering from the complexities of this one topic to write a movie about it. Don't hire them if you can't fire them. It's a requisite to healthy management.

What does a healthy, evolving individual look like?

1. Challenged.

A healthy evolving person always has too much to do, and not enough time to do it. Remembering that Nature seeks balance but rarely stays balanced, so, it's a continual struggle for the healthy individual to fit life into the time.

2. Disciplined.

Clear and unbendable boundaries around time, quality and effort make the healthy, evolving individual easy to be around. They might be challenged, but they are inventive, creative and relaxed enough to, leave the office on time, arrive at appointments on time, get home on time and to produce good results. It's all about frameworks and these drive creative management.

3. Enthusiasm.

Healthy, evolving people are keen to do more. It's a burning desire to do more in less time. A real desire to do it faster, easier, more and with less energy. There's no pulling back or contraction, it's 100% commitment to work, love and life. That's evolution.

# Unhealthy - UNFIT - Organisations

When strategy, structure and culture don't FIT, there's disharmony, and this manifests itself in obvious ways.

What does an UNFIT Organisation look like?

1. Broke.

When the money dries up, it reveals a lack of evolution in the process, product and effectiveness of the business. In this day of smart business, you'd have a 99% probability of being on target if you looked for the cause in the culture. When people don't change their mind, businesses fail.

2. Having emotional fights.

Whether people argue silently, or scream and shout, it doesn't make any difference. Extreme emotional violence and abusive language is a great signal that strategy, structure and culture are out of FIT. It's more difficult to point the bone at the culture as the only source of this UNFIT situation especially in smaller organisations when the boss might just have the resources and strategy messed up.

3. Flooded with customer complaints - Quality Issues.

The most revealing external indicator of a declining FIT between strategy, structure and culture is revealed in quality control issues and rise in customer service complaints. This includes quarrels with clients and contractual arguments. This is an absolute no brainer to direct the issue to the culture. The primary cause of this culture problem is a lack of respect from leadership for the current cultural lock up. When cultures get locked up, either by union resistance to change or by a pervading uncertainty in the future, mindless managers will often re think the market strategy without consultation with the stakeholders at a culture level. It's a naive business approach that can set out to change the marketing and corporate strategy of the organisation with little or no respect for the human reality. Remembering there are only three ways for fast culture change when people don't have evolving skill. Shock, shock and shock, all of which hurt people unnecessarily.

# UNFIT For Work - People Problems

When disharmony strikes at an organisational level, and reveals itself in UNFIT organisational signs, the people within that organisation have been struggling for a long time already. In other words, the real first sign of an UNFIT organisation is UNFIT people, people problems.

What does an UNFIT for work person look like?

1. Becalmed.

Intensity is the key to a full, evolving life. A person with not enough work, walks slow, talks a lot, wastes time, emotionalised, makes mountains out of mole hills, and gets themselves into a flap about their private life. Problems expand to fill the time we give them, and when there's not enough discipline or intensity for work, then people gravitate to low priorities.

2. Forgetful.

When a person is not showing up enthusiastic for their job, their mind becomes mush. Mushy minds drop things, forget things, and most often closed to new things. Forgetful minds are undisciplined minds. A short pencil is better than a long memory.

3. Ill-health.

Tiredness, exhaustion, colds and flu are just the tip of the list. Heart attacks, strokes and more are the other end. When our competence to manage ourselves is less than what the company demands, we get ill. This is like closing the gate once the horse has bolted. Instead of evolving and growing skills for self-management, many people strap themselves in with old work practices, with old work ways, with old thinking and then try to drive harder. The loss of wellness is a real indication of blocked personal and business growth. It's Nature's last resort.

# Leadership through Change

If people don't trust the organisation's strategy, then they will not change their culture. When it comes time for culture change in an organisation where leadership has not shown good judgement in the past, people fear the consequences; they stop growing because they don't trust the leadership. They protect their heart and resist. It's human and natural to do so. Why should a person trust that the future would be better than the present? They've made a comfort zone right where they are. Why change?

If there is a lack of trust in leadership due to past bad experience or a history of bad leadership, then the tables are flipped. The culture is fixed until confidence is restored and there are only three ways of achieving that end. Two are painful, one is slower.

The first painful way to restore faith in leadership is through a take over by a highly resourced organisation in which it consumes the smaller one and all it's uncertainty into it's larger mass. It's like a lion eating a rabbit. No more rabbit problem. There will be attrition at a human level here. The old senior management team of the smaller company will be like the bones of the rabbit. Indigestable. They won't be welcome in the new structure.

The second painful way to restore faith in leadership is to change it. That means, changing the senior team, especially the CEO. The reason this is painful for more than just the old CEO is that many people work for companies because they like the leadership style, they'll all probably need to leave as well.

The third way of restoring faith in leadership is to inject a massive amount of resource in the organisation to make the probability of success with the existing leadership, go up. Of course, some of that resource will line the pockets of the culture team to soften their resistance and erase their memory. But as any leader knows, it doesn't take much bad news to sour the milk once it's been soured before. People remember the taste of yesterday all too well. Again, it often results in a more authentic approach like change the team or change the leader. Resistant cultures that don't trust leaders rarely move by promises. They want results and results only come when they move.

# Why Innerwealth?

The more a person understands themselves the faster they adapt to change. The more enlightened people don't make a stand, so, for them adaptation is the key to happiness. They are never disturbed.

There are many forms of self-awareness but most of these confuse the development of a "good personality" with "self-awareness." Unfortunately, the more we develop that personality, the more resistant we become to change.

The Universal Laws of Nature provide a unique platform for self-awareness because they confound the idea that we have a fixed and identifiable identity that's real. The Laws of Nature align the human condition with Nature and Nature is always evolving.

Truly, the capacity to adapt to change is one of the most vital outcomes of self-growth. Anything that tries to "lock in" some form of value set or belief set is the opposite to self-awareness. It's more likely to be ego development and this is what blocks change.

Innerwealth means we understand the great powers that exist within us. They begin with the power to manifest and end with the power to stay centred while all around us goes into turbulence.

However, Innerwealth's greatest contribution is the tools to help people grow, evolve and build on challenge. This is absolutely unique to this process. When you understand how to build and expand your Innerwealth based on the challenges and chaos of your life, you'll jump into work and life with far less conservative restraint.

We grow at the border of order and chaos. So, it's wise to adopt a philosophy for your life management that includes a continuous cyclic stream of challenges. The idea of finding a sustainable peace is nonsensical, instead, Innerwealth process offers you ways to continually move from the inevitable chaos, back to order easily. We can call this the real melody of life, harmony.

If you can grow from challenge, you'll embrace it. You will celebrate and not blame but thank people for challenging you.

# The Human Awareness

We often talk about organisational culture as if it's an ocean in which fish swim, or people exist. But it isn't that at all. Culture is people. Many of them, thinking the same sometimes, thinking different at other times. The net result of the individual thinking process from one or ten million people is a culture.

Families have cultures. Businesses have cultures. Communities have cultures. Whole nations have cultures. In Australia we're proud of the Aussie culture, "put another shrimp on the barbie, mate."

Advertising gurus tap into our sense of belonging to sub-cultures. They sell cars, washing powders, toothpaste and holidays based on our sense of belonging to a culture. Like the green movement, it's a global culture.

Innerwealth is a culture too. It's a universal culture. The laws that run the green culture are, "save the planet" but the laws that run Innerwealth culture are the universal Laws of Nature.

The importance of Innerwealth culture for business change is vital. You can't manage anything you can't see the balance in, so, by expanding awareness we help people manage larger and larger entities.

When you're a child you manage yourself. When you're a parent you manage a family. When you are first in business you might manage a department, then a region, than a larger region until you become a global manager for something. With each expansion in responsibility comes an expansion in consciousness, otherwise we fail.

If a person who is only aware enough to manage a region becomes a global manager they'll stress out and fail, or be forced to evolve very quickly. The key here is that the person who manages something well sees both sides to it. The person, who remains calm even during family drama, can see both sides to family issues.

Innerwealth uses the Laws of Nature to evolve our consciousness; it makes us more open to change, more expanded because we see things from a bigger perspective. Little things don't bother us.

# Skills for an Evolving Workplace

When it comes to building an evolving organisation that is a living, breathing, growing entity there in no better place to start than by understanding its Nature through the Laws of Nature. There are five laws.

Law 1. The Law of Balance.

The law of balance gives leaders wisdom, controls emotion, helps people make wise decisions, increases capacity to include diversity, saves time, builds stability and, prevents domestic disaster as a result of UNFIT business.

Law 2. The Law of Evolution.

The law of evolution explains everything in business. It is a model for personal and business achievement. It resolves conflict, helps people communicate, turn up at work fully present and sets a benchmark for sustainable profit. It prevents failure and gives peace of mind.

Law 3. The Law of Interconnectedness.

This law of interconnectedness leads to inner peace, good human relations, abundant thinking, and social ethics in business. It prevents blame, victim and judgemental cultures. This law opens up the limitless possibilities of the human condition.

Law 4. The Law of Harmony.

The law of harmony puts discipline around our work life mindset. It introduces us to deep insight into good human communication, marketing, human relations, health and wellness. It is an important law for leaders to follow.

Law 5. The Law of the One and the Many.

The law of the one and the many explains hierarchy, structure, strategy, and organisational change. It reveals the secrets of success, marketing, client management and authority in work life management. It helps people understand the human dynamic perfectly.

# The Four Important Keys for the Future

New leadership needs cultures that change fast. We've pointed out that competitive organisations change their strategy over a weekend and to implement that change the culture has to change just as fast.

Good leadership needs organisations that want to adapt to change fast, and this means always looking for better ways to do things.

**Fast Culture - Adaptability.**

Even the best leader will fail if their organisation cannot adapt to change. The driving force of success for a leader is to be able to move the strategy and have the organisation move with it. This is the first step.

**Fast Culture - Evolving Culture**

By fixing the time we allocate to work we force ourselves to ask the evolving question, "How do I get more done in less time." By a simple focus on efficiency, we draw our attention to improving productive work time, process and behaviour.

**Fast Culture - Good Self-management**

We ask what we are responsible for, we ask what we need to do to fulfil that, we create four priorities, and we do those. Everything else we dump or delegate. This is how we refine our own valued work practices. Working on low priority tasks lowers our Innerwealth.

**Fast Culture - Work-Life Balance**

We set standards for our health, our relationship and our Innerwealth and we uphold these at all cost. We work to cause these things to be at their best. No compromise - no excuses.

# Adaptability

There's a new independence in people at work. They need more, can do more, and demand more individualised leadership. The power for change is in the hands of the individual. Leadership must adapt to it.

People come to work to live their dream, and when they don't they sabotage. A collage of competing individual forces faces a leader now. People want, and demand their human right to enjoy their work and those competing forces need a new approach to management.

If we acknowledge the human right to enjoy our work, we must also acknowledge the fact that people are expendable. If the skill of the individual, and their capacity to evolve with the organisation is not there, then, we are paying a high price for their services.

It's two sided. People are demanding more from their work-life, and organisations need to support that. However, organisations are also demanding more from people, there is an intensity building and only the fittest will survive.

Current self-management practices are inadequate. We've gone through psychological models of behavioural modelling, the use of Eastern arts as a counter balance measure and now, there's a fashion trend for health spa's and recovery clinics. None of this will sustain the required levels of self-mastery for individuals, leaders and teams to move into the future without increased drug support, family breakdowns or a lowering of customer service values. None of these options fits with the evolution Nature demands.

Nature is, the best management model you'll ever study because it's all about refinement of process, ways to evolve from where you are into the future, how do get more done in less time. This model, however, has some challenges for the individual and the leader. It requires people to deal with their emotions, to bend their identity, to be flexible in their mindset and to question their ego stance in wanting to be right. Here's a model that leaders can use to grow their organisations but there's going to be resistance at some fundamentalist levels.

The challenge for leadership in the future is the human mindset.

# Evolving Culture

The question that must be asked for a person and a culture to evolve at the pace of strategy is: How do we do more work in less time? The world is moving at a million miles an hour. Sometimes we're standing still and life is rushing past us. It seems like we can lose touch with the beauty and peace of life if we don't take control of time.

This is the best question a leader can ask everyday, "What are you doing and how can you do it better and in less time." The sign of a bad manager and therefore a bad leader is when jobs that should take 10 minutes take an hour. And an even worse sign is when jobs that took an hour last year, take an hour this year. It takes a keep eye for detail but we need to be adding work volume to our day, by reducing the time we take to do it, not reducing workload in order to cope with our inability to evolve to higher levels of skill.

People who leave the office late, in an evolving culture are the poor leaders, the poor managers. Which is going to challenge some paradigms, especially in Japan where the top guy works the longest hours, even if he or she doesn't need to.

Work expands to fill the time allotted to it. So, we allot less time. We simply evolve our process, our thinking, our systems. If it took an hour a year ago, then it should be taking 45 minutes or less now. Eventually, we automate it.

All the existing jobs that you know in the world will be redundant within 10 years. We need new job titles because we're automating the old ones and doing away with them. So, up skilling is a key security measure for those wanting to remain employable.

Doing more in less time means we are going to have more time and the question is going to be asked about what we do with that time. One of the major reasons cultures get stuck and leaders can't lead is because people are protecting their butt by holding resistance to change. Those days are coming to an end, beware.

# Self-management

People who work on low priorities get paid what they are worth. We get paid for the level of our priorities.

People who work on low priorities beat themselves up at home because they feel devalued. They've devalued themselves by working on low priorities.

My estimate is that most people I meet at work could radically increase their productivity if they just worked on high priorities and either delegated or dumped the rest.

When we work on high priorities it forces us to manage our workflow in a much more creative and innovative way. We're always looking for ways to focus on the important things.

When we do culture change in an organisation we ask each individual to agree on their three highest priorities in their job. You'd be surprised at the contradictions between what people think are their top three priorities and what they are actually held accountable for.

To work inspired, to feel great about yourself at work it is absolutely essential that you work on high priorities in the context of the organisations needs, and make sure they are the same as yours. Remember, what for one person is a low priority, is for another person a high priority. For example: doing your tax return might not be your highest priority but for your bookkeeper it's 100% top shelf.

Priorities are one of the most important skills of good productivity. It is also the most important boundary for evolution in an organisation's culture. A leader cannot get an organisation's culture to match the strategy if people are content to determine their own priorities and therefore have no real investment in change.

# Work-Life Balance

One of the untouched domains of organisational culture change is people's domestic privacy. This is a healthy no go zone for people who don't trust managers or management to maintain a professional and private gap between what is shared and what is made public.

However, domestic circumstances are affected by and cause huge effect on work culture. People who are depressed at home often bring it to work and either react to it in aggressive communication or, fall into sloth.

One of the key skills we might share as part of the Laws of Nature culture change program is the skill of creating great relationships at home. We're not afraid to cross that boundary however we do respect people's right to not invest too much of their privacy in this area of their corporate program.

Many people expand their work as a substitute for love. When relationships begin to sour, or get past their use by date, people begin to compensate and those compensations usually lead to some rather irrational behaviour. Because people can keep their private life private we're often faced with resistance that is not, at first, rational.

We encourage clients to think holistically and in doing so, to consider the compartmentalising of the areas of their life as an emergency strategy rather than the norm for a healthy balance.

Disharmony at work can affect people at home. Disharmony at home can affect people at work. We make this link very clear and help people understand that even when they think they've quarantined their issues; it is very unlikely that they don't have leakage from one to the other.

The real issue is not that relationships affect work or work affects relationships, the real issue is how long it goes on for. A few days here and there of drama at home might cost us a few days at work or a few days at work might catch us unaware and accidently come home. But if it goes on for weeks or months, there's going to be a real loss of focus, drop in priorities and long-term negative consequences.

# Summary

The world is changing faster and faster and people in business are struggling to keep up. When people struggle to keep pace with change, either the change doesn't happen, or the people hurt. In business this is disharmony and potential failure.

We've introduced the topic of FIT for work. It asks whether the Strategy, Structure and Culture of any organisation are in FIT with each other. Classically, Strategy takes a day to change, Structure takes a month at most and Culture has taken years. The way Nature deals with this MISFIT - is by introducing a shock.

Culture shocks move organisations and their people into the future fast. People will change if there's no choice and a culture shock is that lack of choice, the Tsunami a business doesn't want to have.

We look at two main culture shocks. The first is a big chequebook: classically it's called a downsize. In this, typically you fire half the staff, and pay the rest the money you were paying those who left. This is by far the fastest and most simple culture change mechanism. However, it has obvious high human cost. It is the model of choice for most entrepreneurs who buy, sell or merge business.

The second method Nature employs to cause a culture shock and therefore move cultures into pace with strategy and structure changes is to dry up resources. In Nature, draughts, floods, fire, tsunami cause rapid environmental change, and, in spite of our human compassion, those changes are obviously long overdue. So, when humans are out of step with Nature's evolution, expect disaster. In an organisational sense this is bankruptcy, lost market, poor profit, emotional drama.

The final method is to evolve-ya-bastard. This is the method Innerwealth uses to cause culture change fast. The key to it is to acknowledge that cultures are just large groups of independent people and that to change that culture fast, each individual needs to be willing to grow, skilled at growing and focussed on evolving.

There's no room in a fast changing organisation for people with their foot on the brake. The key is to ask how do I do more in less time.

# Chapter 2.
# Nature At Work
# Nature's Wisdom

When you run your fingers over the solid trunk of a tree, pick up a stone and notice its aged patterns, examine the fragility of a leaf, and let water flow through your fingers you are doing the best MBA on earth. No fancy trends or academic hoo haa. Don't mess with Nature she's an impossible fight to win.

# In Australia We Say, "G'day"

It means have a wonderful, amazing, fantastic, superb, sensational day. We just understate it a bit. In the countryside, having a great day is pretty normal because we don't have fancy theories of what makes a soul or a spirit or a God or anything like that. We just look at the stars and we recognise it.

It's hard to teach city people about these things because they always ask, "why?" They are very inquisitive people because for them, to know something, they have to analyse the daylights out of it. We don't.

We just look into the campfire and there's all the answers right there. The aboriginal people say that the bush talks and the fire talks and the city people ask, "what does it say?" and the old wise aboriginal man can't believe his ears. He laughs so hard he falls off his little log and rolls in the dirt. He can't stand up, he's laughing so hard. "What does it say?"

Then he gets up, puts on a straight face and says, "oh, the fire is talking now, It says hello, how are you, where do you come from?" and the city people don't know if he's making a joke. Then the old guy says, "Oh, I hear the tree talking and it's saying, "hey, old fella come here and pee on me." So the old guy gets up and goes off, talking out loud, "ok, I'm coming."

We joke a lot in the bush. But city people don't get the jokes. They say, "why?" and then it's all academic.

In the city we get reality and virtual reality mixed up. We take yoga classes, and medicine, drugs and get absorbed in TV. We can live in a virtual reality world that is so disconnected from Nature that we don't even know who we are anymore.

Instead of standing in the city saying, "gee, I wish I was in Nature," we can say, "I am part of Nature, no matter where I am." That's why the Laws of Nature are really important. They bring us back to reality when we need it.

"Give me a few hours by myself, let me be alone in Nature, shut out all interruptions, and I can bring myself down to my work. It is here that my true Nature and clear thinking comes alive."

Chris Walker

# How to Run a Business

In Australia, the indigenous aboriginal people used to set fire to the bush. They used to set fire to the bush because if they didn't Nature would. They were good leaders because they worked with Nature not against it.

If you run an organisation and you work against Nature, you're fighting against yourself, the world, Nature, creator of Nature and the whole universe. Like that Atlas guy who carried the weight of the world on his shoulders. It's not wise or sustainable.

Money comes in, money goes out; there should be less out than in.

People come to work people go home. People who are happy, work productively. People who are resentful cost a lot of money.

The purpose of a business is to provide people with what they want at a price they want to pay. If a business fails to do so, it won't last for long.

A business that makes things that clients don't want is in trouble.

People don't volunteer to pay bills.

The fun of business management is that it's competitive. Only the FIT survive.

People are always looking for a better product.

Business that doesn't change is called stagnant and in Nature, stagnant things stink. People stay away.

In Nature anything that doesn't adapt, is extinct.

Things can all be explained by recycling. If any energy is not being used to adapt and grow, it gets recycled. It's called death, bankruptcy, divorce.

"The sun, with all those planets revolving around it and dependent on it, can still ripen a bunch of grapes as if it had nothing else in the universe to do."

Galileo

## The Law of Lesser Pissers

If you are out on the farm and the herd is asleep you can do what you want. You can sit and enjoy a good fire. But if the herd is stampeding you better know how to put them first.

In life and business you are going to piss people off. The only questions are who and when.

In self-help it is said that if you are going to piss people off it better be others, because if you piss yourself off, well, life's going to be a struggle. So, that's self-help.

Now, if you come to work and think, the law of lesser pissers, "gee, I can please myself and piss my employees, clients and suppliers off" well you've taken the self-help thing one step too far. Really.

You have to know when you can please yourself and you have to know when the herd is stampeding. One is self, the other is service.

Service is an interesting thing because even the greediest, money-making person is serving. As long as their mission becomes to provide some level of delivery. If your organisation serves people it will succeed. If it doesn't it won't. Now, that service needs to be good, because someone else might be wanting to provide the same thing in a different package. So, that's where happiness comes in.

So, when you are responsible for others you are wise not to piss them off. And when you are just responsible for yourself, then you can piss others off.

In business you are responsible for others and in relationship you have to know which time is which.

This is the key to it. If you are always self serving, then you are going to struggle with looking after the herd, or in city talk, leading.

Victor Frankel reminds us "all things can be taken from us but we are still able to choose the abundance of our heart."

# Growing Pains

Nature never grows in straight lines, she grows between order and chaos. You might say, "so what?"

There's plenty of great business wisdom you can get from just this simple awareness. Let's explore a few:

A period of sustained high growth in the stock market, financial markets, real estate market or your children's height, is going to be followed by a flattening out, or in the case of extremely fast growth, a downturn.

Wealthy people know this, so they invest after the down, and sell before the next one or hold onto property long enough to get the average cycle returns. In other words there's high times and low times and they average out to a medium growth over a long time.

You can translate this into product cycles as well. A product that's growing rapidly in sales is going to flatten out eventually.

Further exploration will take you into office dynamics. Sometimes it's running like a clock and other times there's drama. Of course. Just like Nature. You don't have to react to that, no need to panic. Just come back to the middle path and it'll be ok.

Digging deeper, you can apply this law to your relationships too, sometimes wow, it's fabulous and sometimes, it's ho hum. Remembering the balance of order and chaos - if things are humming along nicely, it's a good time to put on your crash helmet.

Nature evolves everything in the entire universe, including you, at the border of chaos and order. You find those people who are hyperactive and always emotionally off the wall, are also the ones with deep depressions. Uppers equal downers. In between the two, there's growth.

In times of uppers, bank some reserves because when the downer comes you are going to need it.

Evolution does not come from analysing the past. It comes from releasing it.

# Cutting Off Dead Wood

I wish to save people from pain that comes from a huge misinterpretation of the value of a job, and the need to evolve in order to keep that job.

The real essence of organisational performance is natural selection, and anything that blocks this process is a block to good management. What does this mean in real language? It means if people aren't good enough to do their job, they need to be somewhere else.

When a business closes all the staff go elsewhere for jobs. And it's really amazing to see what happens here. Some people were being underutilised, and go out into far higher paid jobs, with much more responsibility. Others struggle. Now, if you are looking for a reason why the business closed, look no further than this fact alone.

Underutilised resources were inside the company so, there was a terrible waste going on, and, dead wood was dragging the organisation down. In Nature, storms blow dead wood off trees. In business it isn't so easy.

I am convinced that organisations these days give people every opportunity not to become dead wood. They train them, teach them, coach them. But some people are dead wood in their personal lives and there's nothing you can do at work to help them with that if they choose not to be helped.

When a person gives up in life, they resign. They resign themselves to easy ways and in a way, put their hand out for others to carry them. Now, some people get a disability, I mean a real one, and they are excused from this; but there are healthy, capable young people who've jumped off the bus and still manage to stay hidden from management. In Nature this doesn't happen. And in business it doesn't happen for long before the organisation starts to sink from all the dead wood.

There are lots of ways for people to avoid becoming dead wood in their own lives and we owe it to them to help them find their bus again, to get a little dream or something and rejoin the real world. If they don't do this they hook into substitutes and resist change.

It is not the absence of possessions that frees a person, quite the opposite. But it is the absence of attachment, the absence of greed and the absence of fear that makes a person happy. Truly a happy person is happy, without anything, and equally happy with everything.

# Leadership

There's a bunch of people sitting out in the forest. A really wealthy guy, a really smart guy, an amazing genius woman, a student, a bushman and an airline pilot. Who leads?

Well you don't know yet, because I didn't tell you the circumstances. So circumstances affect leadership, right because the person who has the greatest certainty in any particular situation, leads.

It's not about words or knowledge it's about the future. If these people are lost, right now, the leader will take them to the future by helping them find their way out. So, the bushman might lead. Now, if they are not lost but they are on a mission to discover a new earth element the genius lady might lead. But, if they are running out of funding, well the wealthy guy might make the best leader at least until the money is in the bank.

You've got to remain humble. That's the key. If you can say, "In this area of my life, that person has more certainty about the future than me," then you can be humble to their guidance. But if they are fluffing around and you don't think they know more than you about the future, they are not your leader.

We need to admit when we need leadership and when we are being leadership. We don't learn from those who follow us, because by necessity anything they are teaching, we already learned. However, we must learn from those who are above us, because they know more about the future than us. They have more certainty.

I know the Laws of Nature like the back of my hand so when it comes to the future for people in the choices they make, I can really lead a lot of people. But if they want help with a heart transplant I wouldn't have a clue. We say, "horses for courses."

“Whoever does not sometime or other give their full and joyous consent to the dreadful scenes of life as well as its beauty can never take possession of the unutterable abundance of power in our existence. They can only skirt the edge and one day will be judged to have neither been alive or dead.”

# Enjoying the Ride

If I go bungee jumping in New Zealand I confess to feeling afraid but I can enjoy it. Why? Because I know the chord is safe. I know that someone understands the rules of engagement.

If I go bungee jumping in a place where I don't understand the safety or the rules of engagement, I have two feelings, one is still fear, but now there's uncertainty, doubt.

Doubt kills the fun of anything. And in Natural Law the whole mission is to eliminate doubt. If you could eliminate doubt form your mind about your business how much fun would it be? It would still be a struggle but struggles without doubts are fantastic and stimulating.

The average person doesn't know it, but there's order in the chaos of life and business. Order meaning that there's a really good explanation for everything that happens. It's like sitting on the moon watching the world go round and smiling, at the beauty of it. Even people panicking about global warming and water shortages have a pattern and seeing that pattern is the mastery you get from Nature's Law.

The pattern confronts our emotion because on one hand life is expendable, and on the other hand we hold onto hopes and dreams and ideas as if they are supreme and the pattern will shift to accommodate us. Observe the pattern, eliminate doubt and enjoy the ride.

The pattern looks like this:

1. There're two sides to everything

2. Everything grows at the border of chaos and order

3. Everything is connected to everything else

4. There's a harmony based on attract and repel

5. All is Hierarchical - Everything is humble to something

I want nothing

I need nothing

And therefore,

I have everything.

# Future Seeing

If you are a leader and someone asks you, "what's going to happen next year?" and you say, "I don't know," then you've shot yourself in the foot.

If you are a leader and someone asks you, "what's going to happen next year?" and you say, "I know that, it's blab blab..." but you really don't have confidence in your answer, then you've shot yourself in the other foot.

Even a squirrel knows to start storing food before winter. A cute little squirrel might have more business acumen than many leaders. If a leader can't predict the future, they're a follower or a bluffer.

Bluffer leaders keep talking about the future, keep drawing plans for the future, keep refining their words and promises for the future, but usually deliver the future only if their luck holds out. Their mission is to motivate themselves and others by bluffing confidence about the future.

Future seeing is the greatest leadership skill there is and it can't be bought, hired, borrowed or faked. It comes from long hours in examination, research and having a beer at the pub. No, that was a joke. But it does also come from associating with people from diverse walks of life and listening.

However, what caps this off is the ability to see 'cause and effect'. If something is happening today, it is the cause and next year there is the effect. So, future seeing is quite predictable really. Once you know and trust the Laws of Nature you see that imbalance today will cause counterbalance in the future. Stagnation today causes drama in the future and lack of respect for hierarchy today causes humility in the future.

Future seeing is the most powerful asset any leader or manager could dream of. And this is what you learn using the Universal Laws of Nature. All eyes are turned to the future. The one who can predict it, has the greatest gift, and will lead the greatest organisation.

Challenge is Nature's way of tapping us on the shoulder saying, "Hey, you, think it through, isn't there a more efficient way of doing this?"

# Environment

There's a lot of blab-blab about the environment at the moment. People are really aware that the environment is so important. There are street protests, TV shows, movies, web sites. My goodness there's a whole industry making money out of improving the environment and as an environmental engineer and ecologist, I'm thrilled.

But it's such an external approach. What about the environment inside ourselves? What about the environment inside an office or more importantly in our homes? What about the environment inside our head?

Once people understood the connection between the way we treat the environment and the way we treat ourselves, but they've lost this awareness. And in offices and organisations this separation is really damaging.

In Nature all things are connected. What we do to, or how we treat this tree, affects how the other tree 200 miles away responds. We're also aware that we are the environment we create. That the boundary between ME and THE WORLD out there, is really just a fictional line in the sand.

Nature teaches us that we are not separate and that the environment in an office or organisation is reflective of the environment we create within. If I am corrupted and dishonest within myself, so, in my organisation, there'll be people to mirror it.

The Laws of Nature also teach us that for every supporter we get as a leader or manager there'll be a challenger. In emotional worlds we look for half-truth, but in harmony with Nature we respect diversity. Supporters and challengers exist in balance in any organisation. What a relief that must be for people pleasers to hear.

Over specialisation leads to extinction. So, those that think emotionally see the challenge and think, "ooh, something is wrong, someone doesn't like me." The generalist sees the dislike and then looks around for the balance of it. It's called consciousness.

Truth is, we can't disconnect from nature. She is us, we are it. All of life is nature, even the good, the bad and the ugly is nature.

If we work in harmony with nature we feel right. If we work against it we feel wrong, disharmony.

Reconnecting means becoming aware of this.

# Reconnect to Nature

While there's a group of people getting wiser, the average city person seems to becoming thicker. That's not suggesting that people aren't more educated, more sophisticated, more discerning and cleverer. But when it comes to living and working happily, people are becoming less aware - unconscious.

Why do I make this statement? Well, once when people were connected to Nature they knew that if they weren't well then they were out of harmony with Nature. That awareness triggered a shift in behaviour and a natural healing would take place. Nowadays, we create a new drug, blame the corporation and join a protest group.

Nature's bible is your body. But this is not just your physical body; a large mass of cells could be called the corporate body too. So, when there's an illness in a body, there's always lots of warning signs, and we do get guidance from Nature. It seems the more intelligent we become the less we listen to Nature's signs and the thicker we become.

Separate anything from Nature and it dies. We have no choice about working in harmony with Nature. And the more competitive a business becomes, the better that harmony needs to be. Alternatively, there're more drugs, pharmaceuticals and stuff to help people stay fixed in their lifestyle, and ignore the signs. With an aging global population the cost of this disharmony is terrible.

Challenge is Nature's way of tapping us on the shoulder saying, "Hey, you, think it through, isn't there a more efficient way of doing this?" When we say, "No, I like doing it this way," Nature gives us a firmer nudge in the form of stress or nervous anxiety or immune system slow down. If we still don't listen to her guidance, we get slugged in the form of a divorce, a health challenge, a business breakdown or a lost job. Nature evolves us. We don't achieve that evolution by backing away from the awareness of Nature, we have to go head first toward it and learn.

# Chapter 3.
# New Leadership
# Walk The Talk

"I would rather have the whole world against me than my own soul."

# Walk the Talk

People want to be led. They want to be guided, and shown the way. People want to be happy, productive and secure. People want to go home to their families and leave their work behind. So, leadership is different now because once upon a time, people came to work, not because they wanted to, but because they had to: if they didn't work, they starved.

Things are different now. People want to be led and they want that leadership to be good. So, those leaders who are still managing in the old style, can still get jobs in third world countries and developing nations, but that's just a few more years of the old school. Once people break through the ground of no choice for work they want new leadership.

New Leaders want new organisations. Great leaders can't stay globally competitive and produce great results if their organisational culture is still operating as if the culture is sacred and change is going to take a mighty force. New leaders need organisations that respond to growth, that evolve fast, that can keep up with the times. So, organisations need great leaders but great leaders need great organisations. It's all a matter of FIT. And in organisations, and leadership, only the FIT survive.

As an evolution agent, I have great empathy for the new challenges for Leadership in organisational growth. On the one hand, people are becoming more independent and socially aware so, they are demanding more socially acceptable workplace dynamics and they need them more than ever before in order to do a good productive day's work. On the other hand, leadership is only as good as the last month or so of performance, so if the organisation doesn't step up, the leader is lost. People are changing their expectations.

More and more, great leadership is about energy. It's about things that can't be owned, touched, spoken or seen. More and more leadership is about unmeasurable quantities like certainty, trust, respect and inspiration. Elements that are communicated non-verbally. Let's explore the opportunities.

# Walk with Heart

It was only 40 years ago, when the great leadership model of the organisational world was to be as "heartless" as possible. People were begging for jobs, much of it was driven by fear and so, being a total bastard was a real positive trait for a good leader. Back then, there were only a few women in leadership roles, so, the macho sporty tough guy usually led organisations in a club clique with like minded buddies. Handshakes in cafes were how much of the business world made the big deals, and the role of the organisation was to churn out whatever was demanded of them. The bully's mentality wove its way all the way down the ranks to the cleaner and coffee lady.

In developing nations there's still a lot of that old style. These countries and their business provide a catch all for Management that hasn't evolved. So, it's still possible to be sexist, abusive and run the old paradigm especially in small business. But it's just not sustainable. It's neither humanly nor financially competitive. As people get a choice about their work life, and as we shift from hard labour to think power, people rightfully demand more evolved leadership.

We need to shift from models of work life that might have been perfect in 1945, when labour was in short supply to a more evolved way of working. Terms like "the art of war" and "doing battle" might be great old business metaphors, but, let's be real, organisational leadership is not the art of war. It's now the art of humanity. Leaders must both be good and do good, if they are going to attract the sort of quality people who can, as a group, stay best of field.

For 30 years leaders have asked me to help them encourage their teams to evolve. With an open heart they have encouraged, cajoled, persuaded, manipulated, motivated, inspired people to adapt to the demands of a faster and faster changing market.

And in situations where resistance is futile, people still resist. Lead with an open heart, don't compromise.

The leaders who've failed over that time have been the nice guys. They are the men and women who want to be liked, who are looking for friendships, who are lonely, who just don't understand the real demands of leadership. They compromised and failed.

# Walk the Right Space

The demands of work now are radically different. Even in the past 10 years, technology has cut a huge amount of human labour and replaced it with machines. Human beings at work are now being asked to do what human beings do best: Think, create, inspire, and innovate. It's all about evolving to higher levels of human consciousness at work.

My dear old dad, used to show me his skills at adding numbers in his mind, he used to show me how clever his filing system was, and how his sales skills were so fantastic. Now, I do all those things in 2 seconds by hitting the save button on my laptop.

To lead people who have to think more, create more and be more inspired is a shift in consciousness. This part of a human is very fragile and it is very easy to get this mixed this up with emotional drama. This new skill set is voluntary, people can't be forced or pressured or coerced into contributing great thoughts. It's a personal contribution people make when they are in the right space and the job of leadership is to create that space.

There are certain essential requisites that make that space. Some of them are environmental, like the right light, the right feel in the office. However, the most critical ingredient that affects the space leaders create for great thinking, higher consciousness work, is the relationship between those people and the leader.

There are four important links that cannot be broken between a team and a leader. If any one of them breaks, it is, in the real world, unrepairable. If a staff loses one of these elements, or is unwilling to give it in the first place, then, that leader and that staff are no longer compatible. One must go and in the case of the compromised leader, that choice wasn't made.

Those four important links are:

# Walk the Four Links

Before we begin to examine the four links between leaders and their teams that are absolutely essential for harmony, higher consciousness work, let me mention that those four links are identical to the ones that make a domestic relationship function in romance.

Link 1. Trust.

Does the leader trust the individual and do the individuals trust the leader? A fragile thread so easily broken. When a leader loses the trust of his or her team, the dynamic is busted. It's hard to repair.

Link 2. Respect.

Once upon a time respect was something we earned but now we know that respect is something we give. All people deserve respect. However, when that respect is blocked in either direction, the dynamic of the leadership is lost.

Link 3. Certainty.

The only reason people need leadership is to give them greater certainty of the future than they already have. A leader who can't authentically promise the future, is not a leader. Uncertainty and leadership are incompatible.

Link 4. Gratitude.

When people start to take their job, their staff, their position or anything for granted, leadership is impossible. Complacency is the single greatest blockage to good leadership on earth.

# Walk Trusted

Sometimes we say things we don't really mean. Sometimes we make promises we can't keep. Sometimes we make mistakes that really affect people's confidence. But all this is more easily forgiven than the greatest trust breaker of all, "When we say one thing and do another."

My first boss used to say, "Don't do what I do, do what I say." and I never, ever trusted him. In fact, I stole from him because I expected him to steal from me. I was just getting even before it happened.

New Leadership trust is one of the most important commodities a leader can have. If there's no trust, the rest is makeshift.

The realisation is that we are really transparent. People who say one thing and do another, are totally bluffing themselves that nobody knows what goes on in their secret moments. Maybe that was true 40 years ago, when people were desperate for jobs and their intuitions were blocked but it is not so now. People can smell a rat. We are transparent and to know that is very important. It means we have to come to terms with our real self, not the false one we think we present to the world.

I work hard, and I play hard. I love the extremes of life. I'm not one for the mediocre life and because of that people can easily misinterpret that I don't walk my talk. I have a disciplined work life and a sometimes undisciplined play life but that's not a real issue as Richard Branson of Virgin fame has proven. He's honest in both places; it's just two different ways of expressing his passion. People trust that.

The real issue of broken trust stems from ethical and moral judgement. If a leader asks for values of honesty, integrity, commitment and solid effort at work but is seen to cheat on his wife, lie to his neighbours or in anyway live a whole different moral code outside the office, people smell it, they won't give 100% trust.

It's the same in a family, parents and children but this is not the venue for that dialogue.

Walk your Talk, be worthy of trust.

# Walk Respected

Respect is something we give and we give it freely. The core of respect is far deeper than what we do. It goes to the heart of what we do.

**Words are Words**
**Ideas are Ideas**
**Thoughts are Thoughts**
**Results are the only Reality**

When it comes to leadership and respect, it's not what you think that matters, and it's not what you intend, it's what you do, and how you do it.

The most successful person who cares little for others will be respected for their success but people will cheer if they fall. The individual who gives respect to others while they achieve success will be celebrated for their success.

Respect is a vital commitment in two directions. From leader to follower and from follower to leader but in each case it is different. The leader respects effort, results and commitment. The follower must respect authority. The authority of the leader is vital to natural structure. If people can't respect the authority of the leader then there is no leadership.

Respect begins with self-respect. When the leader has self-respect they don't do things in private that they would be ashamed of in public. Doing things we are ashamed or guilty of is a complete lack of self-respect.

There are many judgements that can lead to disrespect. People can have a moral high ground and a long memory of the past. People can judge each other and disrespect can follow. This is human and sad, but when there is disrespect for a leader, then there is no leadership. One cannot lead people who do not offer respect. This is true at home and at work. Respect is a vital part of leadership and, apart from prisons and forced labour it cannot be demanded. Lack of respect for leadership is one of the primary causes of business failure.

# Walk Certain

All eyes are turned to the future. The past might be bemoaned, but it is gone. The present is here, it has already made its impact. People are concerned for the future and that is why they look for leadership.

The old leadership was easier, momentum drove business into the future, the market was always to blame for failure and leaders could only provide a nominal advance on that insecurity. People built nest eggs, insured their health, build homes and tried to get them paid off as quickly as they could. The past was an insecure time, and people worked on that.

Now there have been new role models of leadership that have proven themselves immune from markets, and trends, and downturns and raids. They are a tough, no nonsense breed of leaders who have created a new expectation. We can win in any circumstance if we have the right leader for it.

When a leader cannot hold certainty, followers retreat. Whether it's in war, business or relationship. When a person lacks certainty people begin to make fallback plans, growth stalls and the end is predictable.

In business, the quality of leadership is very much a result of the wisdom that leader has in terms of their capacity to guarantee the future, no matter what the circumstance. If a leader has no certainty from their own heart, or from those who control their resources, then that leader is a follower. They cannot lead without certainty.

Blame is the usual process leaders use to excuse themselves from their lack of certainty. They blame head office, or the market or the economy and at a micro scale they blame poor old Pete, who got fired last week. Always blame the last guy.

Real certainty comes from the human heart but it is backed by unemotional wisdom. All uncertainty comes from emotion. No matter how pumped a person is, emotion cannot last, certainty can. In my opinion, the best way to get and hold certainty is to study hard and go bush a lot. Sit under the stars and certainty becomes natural.

# Walk Grateful

People become as we treat them. If you are thankful, they become better. If you are unthankful, they become worse. People become as you treat them and you can't change people. So, you can only thank them and choose the right people for the right job.

Sometimes we think that being critical will help people. We're wrong. Being critical doesn't help people, it just adds to their existing self-doubt.

People become as we treat them. The more we appreciate someone the more they appreciate us. The more we criticise someone the more they doubt us.

We need to see that some people are going to do the job we want and some people are not. That's just how it is. We can appreciate everyone but do they do the right job?

If people don't have the right skills or the willingness to adapt to culture change we don't motivate them by criticism. We get the best out of people and they get the best out of us when we appreciate them.

In the whole universe, what we appreciate grows. Sometimes we split the world into what we appreciate and what we don't, and think that this is going to cause global change. Then we protest. But this is negative and all we do is change the problem from one form to another. We stop the global warming and start some other issue.

Appreciation begins with a light heart. Heavy and critical heart is not going to fix things. It might make hard choices and this is part of life and work but a heavy heart brings things down.

There are always two sides to everything. A negative and a positive. No matter what the situation if you can see both sides, then you have wisdom. If you can see both sides and focus on the good news then you are a leader. This is the essence of people attraction, good service, marketing, sales, healing and communication. There is no half-way story, we find the balance and focus on the good news.

# Walk the Middle Path 1

The old paradigm in leadership meant that the one with the loudest voice, the biggest ambition, the most enthusiasm, and typically the strongest at challenging people to do their best was the leader but this is a style of the past. Now, with inspiration, a whole new world of leadership opens itself.

This is the new leader, the moderator, and the one who can find and stay in the middle path. A balance between forces, one who can see both sides, one who moves forward half way between the pressure of rushing ahead, and staying in the past. The new leader is looking for a sustainable path. We define this as the moderator.

The middle path is the ground between radical rush into the future, and stoic stubborn attachment to the past. In every business these two extremes exist and the one who respects both, and finds the middle ground, is the real leader. This is a major shift from the old school of leadership in which the leader was the one who led from the front, who was the most enthusiastic to go toward the future, the one who made the most noise. They were, in the old school of leadership, the ones who had the biggest ambition, but not any more.

During my MBA, I sat on the board of the University of NSW – Business School. On that board were 12 of Australia's top business minds. Each one was the leader of a huge corporation. They were all high profile and highly inspired people. The Chairman was a shorter, quiet bloke; he too was the CEO of a massive corporation. I wondered how he would chair such a powerful group and what I observed was an exceptional learning experience. He made it his mission to listen to as much of the diversity of opinion on any subject the board discussed. He was the open-minded one who had no opinion of his own, until it was time to wrap up a debate. Then, he'd summarise the room, it made people feel heard and then, with everyone feeling that their opinion was in the melting pot, he'd give a recommendation. He led, he guided the room because he knew all sides, and found a middle path through it.

To be the leader in the new age of business you'll need to find the middle path, firstly in your heart and secondly with others.

# Walk the Middle Path 2

The one who can find the place between too fast and too slow will sustain profits and grow any business or enterprise they start. Entrepreneurs must avoid the extremes. A good entrepreneur might have extreme ambitions but they can't let their emotions get the better of them or they'll lose the support of their team. The best entrepreneur is right in the middle.

Moderating your enthusiasm as an entrepreneur might sound boring but it's not. As part of a complete portfolio, moderation is a sensational ambition that saves you massive amounts of time. Remember always, that the person who goes into change too fast always slows or stumbles eventually. Change means moving forward, and refusal to grow means stuck in the past.

So, the middle path might sound emotionally un-stimulating but remember that emotions are always only half-truths. The middle path is the shortest path eventually. It might sound great to rush into things and experience the highs but it's wiser to pre-empt that, by experiencing the lows before you start.

The most evolved path is the middle path in business. Half way between the excitement of the future potential and practical logistics. One is the father and the other is the mother energy. We need to respect both.

Did you know that we can't manage anything we can't see the balance in? If we see more good than bad we're going to be over enthusiastic and blinded by the rush. On the other hand, if we see more bad than good, we're repelled and going to be stuck in the past. The entrepreneur must not be trapped by either of these possibilities. They are disastrous and lead to failure.

The sustained entrepreneur walks the middle path. This is most important because they celebrate both extremes of radical future and conservative past. It is not a moderation that requires the lack of extremes. The great entrepreneur celebrates both extremes of future vision and conservative wisdom. This is what we call the middle path: celebrating the extremes and letting them balance.

# Walk with Integrity

I was 17 years old. My alcoholic stepmother had just been kicked out of our home and my Dad was still working 6 days a week to pay our way through school. I was desperately trying to graduate to make a return on his years of investment.

But I was living his dream, not mine. I was not really who I was pretending to be and because of this I lived two lives. One that gained public approval and another that was dark and destructive. They were complete opposites. My secret life meant I slid down the drainpipe of my home at night and hung out in street gangs, breaking and entering, steeling cars, vandalizing the whole neighbourhood.

I hated the two faces I presented to my Dad, he deserved better and so, really I hated my life. My integrity was compromised and it took many years to redeem myself. This broken integrity between who I said I was, and who I really was gave me incredible respect for the diversity of humanity, but I was deeply unhappy.

What kept me alive in that time was both my father's and my own love of Nature. Every Sunday for those years I was given a chance to learn to drive up to our remote block of land in the hills outside Melbourne. There we'd chop wood, clean the blackberries from the fences and dig trenches. When I'd done my share, I'd be given the keys to the car to drive around the block. This was the middle ground between the two extremes. Dad actually saved my life with this twist.

The great teacher and philosopher, Osho, once wrote, "the problem with people in our world is that they are on one hand afraid to experience the full madness of their emotion and on the other afraid of the opposite end of life, where there's silence. They get stuck in mediocrity because they can't do anything fully."

Integrity for a new leader means getting beyond faking it. It means that instead of pretending to be one person and thinking that no one knows about the other side, the other extreme, they must realise that people do know about the other side, and it affects respect. People see us, we are not so secretive as we think and when we, like I was as a youth, are out of integrity, we sabotage our business, life and love.

# Walk with Self-guidance

I don't know a lot about other ways for self-guidance. I tried most, they lasted for a while, helped me, but then as I grew, they didn't. Like the old proverb, teachers are made to be stepped on, not stopped on. Therefore, I find it wise to do neither. I am the anti guru - guru. So, the idea of empowering a teacher or guru to me is foreign.

There are four key parts in us that we need to listen to. The first key in my self-guidance process is that I respect myself. There's a spirit inside of me that wants nothing. No ice creams, no cuddles except mine. He's just comfortable or not. I think some people call this intuition. But I don't know about that. I never go against that comfortable - not comfortable guidance from within me.

Then there's mini me. My emotional. My Ego. (Sometimes he's more than mini me) Well I give him some latitude too, but I never, ever respond to him. I let him think the darkest thoughts or the lightest ones, and I just smile as he tries to deal with life and challenge. I feel his state of reaction, attracted and repelled from people but I know he's always wrong; he's only able to see life in half. Never in balance. Never in harmony. Only attracted and repelled. I'm always smiling at his interpretations of life.

Then there's "maxi me." The Anti guru guru. I see love. I love people, and I love life. I love. I don't really want anything, I feel content. I'm not much use to the world because I don't want to fix, change, modify, make better, transform, improve, criticise, save the whales or the rainforest. I love, so how could love be wanting? I hold this love because I know Nature and Nature's Law like the back of my hand. I trust it.

Then, there's my body. Now, this is Nature's bible. If I am pretending all of the above, i.e, I am really listening to my emotion when I say I am listening to my heart, I get sick, ill, tired, diseased, sore, dizzy, fungus, nose bleed, tooth ache.... you know what I mean.

My body is Nature's bible so I learned to read it. That's called Yoga and Body Mind and there're lots of great teachings, some are a bit weak, about this. If I have a sore knee, I know what emotion I am carrying and I deal with it. So, I use my body as a guide to my authenticity.

# Walk with Faith

In one of the most astonishing turns of coincidence I presented a retreat to 100 executives from a multi national money market firm. In my opening statement I said, "there're two sides to everything." With this, one lady jumped up and abused me, "how can there be two sides to everything, my sister has depression?" Then, a small clique of born again religious people walked out, "how can there be a balance of sin and goodness?" The irony was not their reaction but the fact that these leaders were staunch advocates of respecting diversity. So, it seems that they want diversity to embrace their views, but exclude the rest. They didn't even ask, they ran.

Running away from bad news, running toward good news is child's play. And these executives were actually advocating this as the best practice in a multi national firm. This emotional idea is primal at best, inhuman at worst.

What these young, talented, highly skilled and highly paid executives were being taught was righteousness. Stand in one place and things add up to balance, they're wrong. What these people were afraid of was the idea that an assessment of anything could add up to a balance, a null result. How then could they make educated decisions? This was their real fear.

A new leader must look for balance in order to find the inspired path. The inspired path is not right or wrong it's a balance of both. The inspired path is a balance of benefits and drawbacks, pain and pleasure. If you make a choice with that knowledge, no matter what area of your life, you make it with faith. Delusion is thinking that there will be more pleasure than pain, more benefit than drawback, more like than dislike.

I was in Nepal, trekking with a group. They'd paid a lot of money to come this far. I knew it was fine, we trekked higher and higher, everyone was acclimatising well. Then, I knew it wasn't fine. No one was ill. There were as many reasons to go forward as there were to go back. I stopped, found the balance and then listened in the silence. I turned the group around and went back. Half were angry with me - half were happy with me. I suspect that I saved a life that night.

# Bulletproof Jacket

What other people think is complex. Half the energy around you will support you and half will challenge you. This is Nature.

Under that turmoil, your true Nature sits with certainty. That certainty can't be justified. If you try to justify your commitments, they are lies. Your certainty can't be justified or rationalised. It just is.

The more a person justifies their choices the more emotional their choices are. There is no certainty in emotional choices. So, the more we rationalise our choices the more insecure those choices are. Don't follow insecure choices that you make or others make. They are heading up against the current.

Sometimes it just is. Sometimes there are no models or theories, or explanations, or logics. Sometimes you make decisions that later look like mistakes but there are no mistakes unless those decisions were emotional decisions. Then they are emotional mistakes.

One day I made a choice. It was an inspired choice. 2 years later I reversed that choice and people said, "oh, Chris you made a mistake 2 years ago." and I replied, "Maybe, but it was meant to be this way."

Too many people are stuck in their head in their religious, "should do this and shouldn't do that." so their judgements and choices are all made by external rules. If you choose to listen to your innerwealth, then you can use your inner rules for your choices.

Outer rules build our ego. Inner rules build beauty. Only the inner rules can create certainty. Inner rules are intuitions. There is no right or wrong - there is just your choice. No matter how much you think it through, your outer rules can't really defeat Nature. There can be no right without wrong. So, really, outer rules are not authentic.

Your bulletproof jacket must come from your truth. Trust your intuition. Your inner rules are never right and they are never wrong. They are always both. So, it is not necessary for you to defend your inner choices. They are right and they are wrong. Just know it and let the world argue or judge you. Remember, your choice today might evolve tomorrow.

# Walk Intentionally

Inner guidance, inspiration and intuition might be great but they can also be selfish. Therefore, our inner guidance must be achieved with an over riding commitment to do no harm to others.

Doing your best means you follow your inner guidance but you do no harm to others. This is called: Your Good Intention.

Your intent is that your choices will do no harm but they will do harm whether you intend it or not. For every good there is a balance of bad somewhere. So rather than get up on your pedestal and tell the world how good you are, just stay humble and accept there is no good without bad, or bad without good.

That's the reality, no matter what your intention. People have their perceptions and those are always balanced between liking you and what you do, and disliking you and what you do.

Self-esteem means you value the side of you that people like. Self-worth means you accept both sides. To spend the whole of your life defending yourself from the perceptions of people is not healthy. To do your best you are going to have to accept that half the energy of the world will support you, and half will challenge you.

This is why your intent is so important. If you hold integrity in your intention, then the perceptions of others become their right, rather than your guide to your behaviour.

Your intention is your integrity. You must intend no harm. So, you might sell your company or change your job, and some people might get hurt, but you must never wish it, or intend it. Just follow your inspiration and wish everyone well.

So much of life is about accepting rejection. If you can follow your inner guide, then people can reject your choices but not their source, that source is divine. Let your ego go to the wolves for their chewing, they'll be attracted and repelled to your ego. But your inspiration will just be what it is. Nothing to accept nothing to reject - unless you ask for it, and then you know, it's not an inspiration.

## Walk with Trust

In your most natural state you are inspired. Inspiration is not something you do, just like meditation. You can't meditate; you can only place yourself in a position and allow it to happen.

Inspiration is a state of mind and it exists within you 24/7. The only question is whether your emotions are calm enough and your heart focussed enough for you to hear it. The key here is trust.

Worry, stress and fear come from the lack of trust in our natural state of consciousness. If you just let yourself surrender to the forces around you, the path is always clear.

Sometimes we hang onto the past because we don't trust the future. Sometimes we grope into the future, dreaming of better things because we don't trust the past. We have to deal with these things in order to tap our intuitions.

People are different in Nature because life is simple and they trust that. You go into Nature and your intuition becomes your greatest friend. You listen to it, and it guides you. There are no computers or road maps; so, your inner being makes nearly every choice. That's why people are different because they trust themselves and so they become immersed in the beauty of the forest or a magnificent sunset. In Nature people think differently and no matter what life they lead, they find peace in Nature.

Amongst the computers, mobile phones the rush can overwhelm us and then all that is left, as a basis for decision-making is our intellect. This intellect will appeal for approval from people and you can't trust that.

So, building self-trust includes creating a deep self-awareness that can be achieved in Nature. If you can learn the Laws of Nature you'll be able to bring that awareness home with you too. Ask always the question, "where is God not?" Nature, you will see, is everywhere. It's just a matter of understanding and awareness and this is how you get to build trust.

# Walk Enlightened

I had read enough ancient Yogi texts to know that love expanded our perception, not contracted it into compartments. But each time I did some sort of self-help I found more rules to add to my existing judgments. Now, I was judging myself for judging myself. Now, with that new awareness I was beating myself up for being attached to things. All the knowledge did was to make it harder for me to turn up at work.

I'd come to work and people wouldn't fit the mould. I'd try to fix them, but thank goodness they resisted. My yoga and meditations and all those things were perfect in their little worlds but I couldn't find a place for them in my work. How could I be enlightened and sell another widget?

I burned the books, tore up my notes, stopped saluting the Sun. I wanted to see, after 25 years of spiritual study who I was if I took off the robes. The answer? Me. I was still Chris. So, then I thought I'll just be good old Chris, and see how that goes, but guess what? It didn't either. I gravitated back to some very destructive behaviour.

Then I gave up. I sulked for a few years and in that time I observed that yoga teachers were competitive and the Guru's played tricks and I thought maybe that's enlightenment too. And suddenly I saw that what exists is perfect. The only thing that needed to change was my expectation.

You see, the universal laws of nature are woven into everything. There's order in the chaos. There's a perfection in everything especially at work. Suddenly I saw the parallels between nature and marketing, branding, product development, conflict, profit, loss, success and failure. Enlightenment is seeing the perfection of it, that's all.

In a little messed up dog eared poetry book I found in a second hand book shop in Manhattan, New York, I read: "I stepped into the water and swam out, I was looking for the other shore, another reality, I swam and I swam, the currents were strong, the sharks gathered, I was lost until there in the distance I saw, the other shore. I reached it, crawled out of the water and there in the sand, leading into the water, my footprints were clear. I was back - I am I."

## Walk with Stillness

To follow your heart you'll need to know how to listen to it. There's a vast difference between emotion and your heart yet, they are hard to separate. To listen to your heart simply find stillness, create order from the chaos.

The person with the greatest certainty leads. It's a relaxed calm... a knowing. This is where greatness begins. We begin to see the future and therefore manifest it. That picture of the future comes from Nature, it conforms to the Laws of Nature, and it is a magnificent vision from within you.

Here's how:

1. Silence
2. Exhale deeply but softly
3. Think Gratitude
4. Let go of hopes and expectations
5. Close your eyes and look within
6. Straight Spine
7. Be perfectly still
8. Ask your heart to reveal its pictures to you
9. Look for details.

# Time out - Be alone

Pascal said, "All human problems stem from the fact that we don't like to be alone, silent in a room by ourselves." I can't vouch for that quote but from the many Zen and Virpassna retreats, I've done, I can honestly say that being alone in a room, with others, in silence is bloody hard work at first.

The great part about being in silence is that you realise how much noise is in your life, and how distracting it is. Almost like running away from ourselves by making noise. Emotional noise, physical noise and life noise itself. So much noise and in the midst of that we're meant to know ourselves?

To do great things in our life we need a strong sense of what we love and what we wish to achieve. We need a strong commitment to our aims, goals and ambitions so that we maintain a good centeredness and personal balance. This is the foundation of all balance. Our own sense of commitment to our dreams, hopes and ambitions. And this means time out, alone in contemplation.

Stillness is a magnificent art. The ability just to sit or lie down with absolute control over our body movement, our mind movement and our emotional movement. Just to observe ourselves in perfect serenity is a profound gift. You can do it simply by going into Nature and enjoying yourself.

Being responsible also means caring for ourselves. On a plane, with your children, if the oxygen mask drops you have to go against all your instincts and put the mask on yourself first. You can't help others if you can't help yourself first.

Get to know yourself each day. Reconnect to your deeper self, your soul. You can do it: it only takes a few minutes but the effect is amazing. Once you reconnect with yourself you'll be able to handle the mad rush of the day easily.

## Walk with a Vision

If you can get out of town for a while and go to Nature, you can create a deep silence and in that silence you'll find your vision for the future.

Now the thing is to bring it back with you and remain flexible about how you do it. My old yoga teacher got a vision to teach yoga when he was 14 years old and followed that vision for 60 years before the west discovered him. For 60 years he just taught classes to local people in the basement of his home. Now he's 90 and smothered in Gold and diamonds. Sixty years, gee, some people can't hold a commitment for 60 minutes.

Trust the process of life. Everything has its time. If you paint, and no one buys your paintings, trust that the next one will have all the learnings of the last one, you are growing toward your destiny as long as you don't question your commitment. You can flex by changing your mediums or your locations but never question the dream.

I'm 55, and people are really surprised because it doesn't feel like I'm 55 because I keep a really big idea about what is possible in my life. I keep reinventing myself and my journey. Sometimes I fail, sometimes I have to adapt to reality, but the dream is always the same. Just the path can shift sometimes.

I meet many clients who have achieved a social and business success far beyond their own childhood dreams and they've hit a plateau. They've sort of flattened out in their life too early and they're old before they hit 40.

Now please don't make a mistake. I am not talking about loud, fanatical, greedy money hunger. I'm talking about a dream to leave a mark, to create something that will make the world a better place. You know we're all going to push up daisies eventually. And even a great individual will be forgotten after a few generations. So, why not live with love and follow your star, make the journey worth the effort and inspire a few people along the way?

## Walk Present

Anything we do begrudgingly, we sabotage. So, no matter what task it is, even if you don't like it, there's a way for 'spinning it" in your mind to make it good to do. That's self-mastery.

To avoid self-sabotage means that everything you do is done with presence: you do it without begrudging it. By doing everything with total presence, you get lost doing it, time goes away, the need for food or comfort vanishes and you are just doing it. It can be changing the most disgusting nappy but if you love that child you don't even care. You aren't there for yourself - you are "turning up" for the baby.

If you do anything, I mean anything in your life where you are not turning up 100%, you're actually wasting your time. It means to do something well with total commitment. You simply "turn up" 100%.

Anything you can't link to your values, you sabotage either subconsciously or consciously. I used to play football, Aussie rules, and I really wanted to be a hero in that sport, but I loved playing it, not all the fights and aggression that goes with it. So, I sabotaged myself. I got more and more injuries, until I quit. Sprained ankles are the most telling self sabotage mechanism in sport. It really shows us with our head in one place and our body in another. (This is the meaning of self-sabotage.)

One great technique to bring your body and your mind into unison is to always do whatever it is you are doing with 100% commitment. And, if you can't, don't do it. This will save you so many car accidents, business losses, relationship failures and health problems. If you are going to drink or smoke or make love or do anything in your life, even going for a walk, do it with 100% conviction or not at all.

It's when we're half hearted that things go sour. I remember my first solo flight in my glider. I was ready to do it technically, but emotionally I didn't feel right. The instructor got out of the training plane and re fastened the canopy. Next thing I was at 3,000 feet and gliding home. I was ready, but not 100% committed. I came so close to a disaster because when I needed to commit to my landing, I only half did it. I drifted off the runway and only through luck, landed safely.

## Walk with Conviction

We cause ourselves a lot of pain and regret because of ignorance and inexperience. For example: We think that our relationships will survive no matter what we do. But as divorce rates rise, people suddenly see that little bits of compromise five years ago, turn into disasters now. So, what we need is wisdom, right now, before problems start.

That's what I believe we get by staying connected to the earth, to Nature. Instead of philosophising about energy and karma and all sorts of psychological mumbo jumbo, it might be better for some people just to go out into Nature a bit more. We are really wise, when we take off our ego and this is what we get from a good healthy relationship with Nature.

When you go into Nature, after just a short time you start to develop a love for all the small things. It keeps us humble and this in itself is really special. In the rush of work we can lose that simple appreciation all to quickly and our ego can take over. We start to take too much for granted. This is ignorance.

By fixing a daily discipline you free yourself. I know it sounds like a daily discipline might be restrictive but it isn't. Freedom means the ability to make diverse choices and to do what ever you do with total conviction. Freedom is not the ability to throw care to the wind and be reckless, that just leads to limitation.

What you eat today, think today, do today, creates your tomorrow. So, there's no real use in worrying about the now, it got created by yesterday. Discipline means that you choose what you eat, do, think now based on how you wish to feel tomorrow. On the other hand if you throw care to the wind and eat, do, think today what you feel like, then tomorrow usually suffers. A hangover is a good example.

It's hard to do good if you don't feel good. So, a significant part of balance is about our commitment to ourselves. Our authenticity to self. We can compromise at work, this is obvious, but if we compromise to ourselves, it is not always so obvious, yet, it is more damaging than anything, even more than compromising a relationship.

# Walk Kindly

Conventional wisdom will suggest that if a person is doing their job well then no mistakes will emanate from their management. If you look at our government system, the minister is often held responsible for mistakes that happen within their department. Most often the opposition, playing on this conventional thinking, will call for the minister's resignation.

Nature's Law predicts reality. Good managers rise to their level of incompetence. This alone – the witnessing of incompetence can prove that a person is evolving through their work life and it is this incompetence that needs to be honoured as a great sign of someone "working hard" to grow their work. Mistakes, errors in judgement are natural but only if a person or their organization is growing. A leader who asks for growth in their organization, but punishes incompetence has created a really stupid conflict in their signals. Actually, it needs to be something we become proud of, and something we embrace in our process so this internal growth doesn't flow on to the client.

# Walk Independently

At work, it's the unspoken norms that affect you more than any other aspect of business culture in either promoting or negating your mindset. You are not a victim unless you either choose to be oblivious to the unspoken cultural norms or, you respond and conform to them. "Ugly minded" people are always looking for recruits. Their world is fearful and lonely so, they look for comrades. Don't fight them, or reject them, have compassion. The beautiful mind doesn't judge or reject it just doesn't buy in.

Do an experiment that I often do in corporate training. Place a picture of something really bad in front of you while you do your work. Even write a negative word like "hate" on a piece of paper, and put it way over on the side of your desk for the day. And see how much the triggers from your environment affect you. Put a motivational picture of a racing car nearby, and see how it wastes your time. Now, as an alternative, put a pot plant, a bunch of fresh flowers or a picture of your children nearby. Something that softens you and then see how it affects you. Environments are the beginning of beautiful mindsets, but only just the start.

Waiting for positive feedback is childish. Children want approval and deserve it, because they are too young to self manage. You're not. So, approve of yourself, accept your mistakes, learn from them, and acknowledge your courage, commitment, love, support and all the positive half of the whole truth. Now, be careful. There's two sides to everyone, so please, don't start fluffing your feathers. Simply acknowledge that there are two sides of your competence and your personality, but focus on the bright side. That's the key.

# Walk with Love

If you can love your work the work will love you back.

The old paradigm encouraged people to love the company. The new paradigm says love your work.

The love of anything does not mean, peace or the lack of challenge but rather it means the willingness to give your all to it, regardless.

To love anything, especially your work, you'll need to welcome the good news and the bad news with the same enthusiasm. Support and challenge are two halves of love. The ego wants support, peace, and happiness, nice flower, power. This is the ego, wanting to become the God you worship. Me, my, I, us, me. The desire for pleasure is the desire for bliss, wealth, comfort, goodness and self-preservation. The real worship of a higher power comes from action. When we can embrace challenge and destruction with the same energy that we celebrate creation, we know God. In the real world it means having a purpose in life greater than self-satisfaction.

Never let a relationship, a job, the world or a friend kill your commitment to live life to the best and highest degree, in other words to "Live with Spirit. Be relentless in your pursuit of perfection and know that rigidity, hardness and aggression destroy happiness.

## Walk with Spirit

There are a million distractions, a million things you can do each day. Your energy, your time, your investment in doing this is your real spirit in life. To value your spirit value your time. To value your time you'll need to work out your top 4 priorities and make sure you focus your effort on those. Remember, the pain of regret outweighs the pain of discipline.

Living with an open heart means living in harmony with Nature. To grow, evolve and flex means you learn to adapt to situations no matter what the circumstances are.

You'll need to see that sitting on a pillow with your eyes closed, miles away from the real world of relationships and work is no great achievement. Enlightened means walking down the main street of some wild city somewhere in the world with a loving smile in your heart.

It's a commitment to a quality of work and life to hold your heart open and live inspired. All it takes is the awareness of the real meditation behind the emotional veil of life itself. This is not a full time occupation. Sometimes our emotions are just the way we like it, but please remember that Nature's first Universal Law offers you the insight to know that emotions that go up, breed emotions that go down.

Meditation cushions are addictive: It is so easy to find a bliss on a cushion, and then judge the outside world as bad because it destroys your peace. This is foolish philosophy, to put yourself in a bubble and resent the reality of the world. There are many yogis' who hate the commercial world, hate the evolution of rain forest. They are in some form of "yoga bubble" and they don't want it burst. This only breeds judgement instead of learning love.

Living with spirit means loving life no matter what happens.

# Walk Realistically

So many HR managers in the world are really hippies in disguise. They really want a flower power peace to descend over the earth and in particular the organisation that has become their mini world. I get it and it's a magnificent contribution with meditation rooms, yoga classes and all sorts of relaxation techniques they really improve the health of the individual. But what is the cost?

The growth of any organization occurs at the border of chaos and order. And as much as we'd all love everyone to agree with us, they don't. If people agree with us 100% - then we can be sure that we've just intimidated or tricked 50% of the real story to go into subterfuge. People bite their tongue when there's need for agreement, they want promotion, they want to be liked by HR or they just can't be bothered arguing with you. Usually the latter because you've done the "communication skills workshop," and you know how to "get people onboard." Rubbish!

Real people disagree at least half the time. Or better put, real people disagree at least half the energy they share. Maybe 99% of the time they agree but that 1% is going to be a total bun fight. Take the idea outside the workplace and remember a relationship you had or have where you and your partner agreed to agree. All is great until that one, usually trivial matter sparks world war three. All that collusion counterbalanced by one single bun fight. This is natural, it's not what religious or philosophical ideals encourage, but it's real life and it's totally unavoidable and predictable.

The chairperson must encourage conflict, and disagreement that really gets all the fact out on the table. By the end of any meeting the chairperson should in theory, have a balance of information gathered from the table that is absolutely deadlocked. This is why there's a chairperson. Real meetings must become deadlocked. The information for something must be equal to the information against something for a wise decision to be made.

# Walk Revived

Coffee, pressure, transport, decisions, people, stress: tension.

Alcohol, food, television, sleep, massage: Time Out.

Deep breathing, swimming, jogging, yoga, meditation: Relaxation.

TV is not relaxation. Play station is not relaxation. Reading a novel is not relaxation. These are wonderful enjoyments, entertainments, fun things to do and really nice, but just like chicken chowmein you might eat from a street vendor in Kathmandu, what makes you feel good in the short term isn't always going to be good for you tomorrow.

Real relaxation, like meditation or yoga requires a significant physical blowout, so there's blood pumping through your veins and then time to calm the nerves. Like going for a jog, then coming home, stretching then lying in the corpse pose for 10 minutes. Too many people take the corpse pose too seriously. They come home from work feeling like a corpse, then lie down like a corpse and then eat a dead corpse before doing the corpse TV before bed. This is the beginning of ill health. Real relaxation – after some form of heart stimulating exercise need only take 15 minutes a day for total nerve soothing.

Like food, our sleep patterns change as our work demands change. In winter we sleep more and in summer less. Good healthy sleep is a science and we do well to learn that art. It's not the hours of sleep that are as important as the quality of it. Good sleep is important for recovery.

# Walk in Peace

If we are unhappy, it is because we want what we haven't got. It is so simple. There is no other trigger for unhappiness. And when we compromise happiness most other things that we want, like good friendships, deep relationships, personal success and compassion go out the door with it. So, a no-compromise zone for life balance might be happiness that comes with contentment.

This is a very potent place to begin your day. It starts with the affirmation, "I am happy, no matter what." Can you imagine the shift in your life if your mind stayed calm and your heart stayed open, even if the sun rose in the West? Nothing can stop you, no one can take your power because you are content.

When I take stressed people into the bush, they drop years off their face. They become vital and their sense of humour comes back. They relax into awareness and start to smell the roses (or gum tree) again. There are many reasons, but one of the most profound is that when people go into the bush, they leave their worries behind. They forget their "wants" and start to celebrate what's in front of them right now.

I've seen grown people cry more often in the bush than anywhere else. They cry because they realise what an ass they have been. They realise that all they have been doing to their loved ones, their work colleagues and themselves is putting pressure on. They've just forgotten for a while, how to be happy. But it's never lost, just overwhelmed by wanting.

People really are extremely beautiful when they let go of all the worry and wanting. My father used to say, "90% of what I worried about, never happened. And the other 10% didn't change even though I worried about it." He'd shrug and smile. I think it was his way of imparting some wisdom.

# Walk with Calm

Be early for breakfast, be early for the bus, be early into work, be early into meetings and be early getting home. Be early to the gym, be early for the flight. I am the earliest person I know. I always have a note pad, and something to write with so, early doesn't mean waste, it means prepare, arrive, and relax.

The person who rushes here and rushes there because they are late is triggering all sorts of primal levels of chemistry in their body. They'll be causing premature aging, nervous complaints, emotion and irrational thought.

The leaders who command respect are not running for the train or panicking about getting out the door on time. They're cool. If you are always running just on time you can plan better, so that your life is more proactive and less intense. That "always running late" intensity can really do some damage to your health and wellness.

Learn to use "waiting time" for your benefit. Learn to meditate while standing waiting, or observe Nature and bring your gratitude to a peak. There's lots of things you can do while you wait. There is really no business respect for late people. Nor is there such a stigma about people who are early as long as you fill the time wisely.

Being in the now might be great. But please remember the Sufi adage, "Trust in Allah, but tie your Camel" The more you have a buffer for things that might come as a shock, the more you can think straight and the more you think straight the more bent can be your creative expression. Plan and prepare for the future.

# Walk Focused

Inner calm is the home of great thought while stress and anxiety is the enemy of it. A person who is excited, anxious or nervous might eventually find the perfect idea, but the journey will be long, expensive and highly disturbing to others. Inner calm is not inner calm. Yes, I wrote that... Inner calm is not the absence of turmoil as many people think. Inner calm is the ability to hold your mind on one topic at a time for a while. Einstein achieved 2 minutes and was proud of it. Some yogis seem to achieve it for a few weeks. The Buddha 7 days. Jesus, 40 days and 40 nights. Inner calm is in the zone, and rather than the complete absence of disturbance it is the prioritization of the one thought focal point, that simply make that thought train a priority and everything else irrelevant. When I am talking to someone I listen. In that time, nothing else exists. Even if there's a phone call or a baby crying I hold focus so that I am present with that person. Even if they lose focus I hold it, until it's no longer appropriate (people often get spooked if you really pay attention to them).

If you are running away from a charging tiger, fear might give you amazing speed, and even clarity of thought. This is the world of the hyperactive child, the ADD individual. There are blessings associated with that mindset because that individual doesn't stop on one spot for too long, they're always free to change the topic, change their body position or change their mood. So, they are free. Really free to think about, act about or talk about whatever comes to mind. That's a nice freedom and it makes it hard for them because no one can keep up, and most people are looking for conventional thought patterns in order to feel comfortable. So there's a lot of stigma around the hyperactive, Attention Deficit individual. But those individuals are teaching us something so important and that is how fast the mind can seek stimulation if things are boring. People who see the solution fast, get bored fast, so they change the topic fast, or move their body. We are all the same. If we're bored, we drift off somewhere else, losing presence and focus. So, ADD individuals are just extremely fast thinkers and instead of drifting into time wasting daydreams, they find new topic of focus. Can you learn from this? Can you see that if you are not invested 100% in whatever you are doing, your mind is going to drift and lose focus. Intensity is a vital key for great thought.

# Walk Quietly

To bring your best mind to life and work means investing more than your logical brain. There are other parts of your mind that, if you include them, can make the situation yours. By trusting your gut feeling, your intuition, you automatically engage your heart and spirit. Inspiration, like the works of Picasso, is just his "gut" feeling at a higher level. So, inspired thought starts at the easy level of trusting your gut and then, with practice becomes absolutely divine. Inspiration is the commitment to follow your own convictions amongst the questions and turbulence of life.

To know this inner self you need quiet, both internally and externally. Your environment must be silent. Many people think that stimulation and great thinking are one in the same, so, they decorate the office with balloons and streamers and child games in order to "inspire" people. But this is very counterproductive.

Great creativity is birthed in complete stillness. All the great thinkers have known this; John Lennon and Miro, Picasso and Pythagoras, Einstein and Elton John, all amazing people, spent or spend, many hours alone, submerging themselves into their work. In my writing and thinking time, I can spend 8 or 9 hours without speaking, no food, nothing, I forget the world, I struggle and wrestle, I stand up and sit down, I go through emotions and my ego screams but eventually, those distractions go away, and my work is really inspiring.

Many great composers and free thinkers have spend time in monasteries or in Nature, alone, in order to become familiar with their inspired side. In our office cultures, we are almost afraid of a moment of silence. Did you know that in a recent study, it was revealed that the average office-working manager, either gets interrupted or actually causes an interruption, every 2 minutes? That's like short grabs of thought in between distractions like the phone, an email, etc. This is not going to make great thinking, and will always guarantee people use time as the resource to improve their productivity.

## Walk It Your Way

To think better at work you also need a real commitment to something bigger than yourself. People who live and work in the now, certainly smell the roses, but they also need a bigger reason, a future perspective in order to stay true to good thinking.

I was sitting in the CEO's office at a Cement plant. We had a contract to supply over 1 million dollars in air filters. I'd been in his home the night before and played cricket with his children in the back yard. During the meeting in the office I suggested to him, "we can drop the air-born particle rate down well below the environmental law if you just upgrade to a higher quality filter, the cost would be around $25,000" (which was for us at cost) I thought he'd jump at the chance given the dust was a real health hazard and each night settled on his car in the driveway of his home. (And therefore in his kids lungs). He refused. I burst into tears. Sounds stupid I know but it just sucked the inspiration right out of my heart.

I knew in that second, that it was time for me to re-engineer my life, I'd just crossed the line, I could no longer pretend that I was living my purpose in this work. In that instant I knew, I had reached the highest level that my business could take me, it was time to sell-up and find my next adventure. Your commitment to your purpose and inspiration and staying in integrity to it, is a value you can hold high and sacred above all else. Otherwise we plateau and self-sabotage our mind and health.

There is a mould a person has to break in order to think better, to be inspired you need to break the mould of conformity. That means you can't think, "I should do this and I shouldn't do that," because this is fitting into patterns of convenience rather than exploring the real potential of situations. Conventional thinking is the mould of fear and impossibilities. Inspired individuals are people who have taken 100% responsibility for getting free of organised and mass consciousness. They know that the world appears to them as they perceive it and if they want to change the world, do something special, they need to think free. Remembering that the way you fall asleep determines the way you wake up is a great clue here. To think great today, you'll need to go to bed with your mind in a really good place. Try – gratitude, presence, certainty and love.

## Walk Inspired

Ask any songwriters, any international composer, and they'll have a list of famous songs they wrote in 3 minutes, or tunes they rattled off in a flash of genius. Yet, they don't make it public because the standard perception is that anything that is created so easily just can't be good. However, genius and great decisions are not about sweat, they are about inspiration, the state of mind we are in when we work.

Trusting ourselves to make short path decisions is a challenge we need to overcome. One client kept employing staff to do research and come up with ideas but 90% of those ideas she already had but didn't trust herself. She was just so reluctant to honour her gift, after being in the industry for nearly 20 years; she still couldn't see how much she'd evolved her talent. She thought she had to sweat and worry in order to achieve creative results. Not so.

If you can evolve your process of "how" you do something, then you can also evolve your process of "why." Inspiration is a mental state that's not really well understood in the business world but totally embraced in the art and sport world. Now, you can't be inspired in a crappy, negative, dark and angry office. You can't be inspired unless you know how to slide you mind into fifth gear.

You have to look inside your own heart and ask what do you love. What are you inspired about? You have to get to the point that what you are inspired about is incorporated into the whole of your life. Linking what you love to what you do is an art. If the race car driver loses inspiration they become cautious and then accidents happen. Inspiration is the motive behind the logic and therefore the race car driver who loses inspiration becomes a nuisance to all the other drivers.

Follow Nature's Law and inspired thinking is natural. There's nothing you have to do to think in an inspired way, is more about what you don't do. You simply eliminate those things that kill your inspiration.

# Walk with a Purpose

When we link what we are doing to something we want, we feel motivated. When we link what we are doing to something we've already got, we're bored.

As a business person you might start off in a job motivated by all sorts of family ambitions or you might want a new car. Even a bad job is good when you have good ambitions and can link them. When the link between what we want and what we are doing gets vague, motivation drops and we start wondering, "Why am I doing this?"

We start with physical motives for work, like money to buy food, shelter and safety. And bit-by-bit we evolve that motive. By borrowing more and more money. We get more and more expenses, buy houses and we can stay in bad jobs a long time using physical motives to link our work to our real desired result.

Eventually, we start to develop some non-material needs. Self worth, pride, satisfaction. Bit by bit we ween the link from money across to other emotional and non-tangible wants that we try to link to our work. If these links don't happen, we find ourselves bored, even as the lead singer of a rock band.

There are so many choices, in the non-material realm. Like a better world, a great education for your children, contributing to humanitarian causes. There's a list as long as your arm but the important ingredient is that the longer you work, the more global will become your concerns.

# Walk with Detachment

The most enthusiastic, energetic people you meet, who live long and are totally happy for most of it, are ambivalent. That doesn't mean bored, it means they are 100% committed to doing great, but aren't too attached to the rewards for it. It's like a violinist; they can either love the playing and be ambivalent to the applause, or love the applause and be ambivalent to the playing. It's hard to do both.

What I'm suggesting here is that you need to invest yourself in self-acknowledgement, (ambivalent to the applause) and commit yourself to doing the best you can. Detachment is a powerful inspiration. It means you can be happy about everything, you can't get too emotionally bent out of shape and, most important, you keep your heart invested, no matter what. The emotional person is attached, and they probably won't like this element at first. Emotional people are run by both positive and negative emotion, so, they flick between "ugly mind" and "beautiful mindset" like a monkey in a tree jumping from branch to branch, attached to this, attached to that. So much energy, so little results.

People are different in Nature. City life is becoming more technology based. People don't even give themselves five minutes to contemplate an apple before they eat it let alone the wonder of Nature.

Touching Nature is important for a "beautiful mindset" to function in our city life. But it's really clumsy if the only time we feel totally balanced is when we're in zone out mode. So, that's why you learn the Laws of Nature because whenever you think like Nature you feel in touch with Nature. That's the rhythm of Nature, harmony. So, if you're in a meeting, sitting at your computer, negotiating a deal over the phone, and you think in harmony with Nature's law, you are at home, beautiful mindset, automatically.

## Walk with Simplicity

One likely thing that can happen when you're bored or burned out is that things start to mount up. You'll notice the housework is not getting done; the office work is not getting done. Your mind will start to add up the list of all the necessary things to do, and at some point go into "overwhelm." Too much to do with too little time to do it.

Overwhelm is horrible. It feels like there are a million options but there's no handle on which one comes first. I sometimes get this when I do my house spring clean. I know everything that has to be done but just can't for the life of me work out where to start. Sometimes it's so weird that I sit down and have a coffee instead. Anywhere to start would be good; instead, I'm looking for the right place, probably wanting to avoid the whole job.

Then, this spring clean takes a funny twist. I'll just throw in the towel and decide to do it tomorrow and be walking past a shelf, see something, clean it up, and next thing you know, the day is past and I've spring cleaned the house. The whole overwhelm is gone, I just needed a kick-start.

Chunk down your list of "to be done" and make them do-able. The most important thing when we are getting our inspiration back is to unblock the pipe, and many times we've stacked all these jobs up, to actually keep the pipe blocked. We stack things up like a mountain of things to do, so we avoid the real issue of not wanting to do anything important at all.

So, at least once everyday clean the desk, forget all your goals and ambitions, clean the whole lot – make your plate completely empty. Either do it, dump it or delegate it. Assign priorities, create an agenda, empty your mind and be as happy as a mouse after a Christmas party in China.

This way, you are going to be clear on how to move forward.

# Walk with Authenticity

The old paradigm of management was to divide work, home, relationship and health into compartments. But we've discovered that this is total rubbish. We might bury some feelings under the carpet when we come to work but this is such a naive understanding of human powers.

People feel our feelings even if we don't reveal them. Our acting can last an hour or so, but no more. People feel our feelings long before we speak them. So, the compartments are purely external.

We fool ourselves when we compartmentalise our life. We think that no one knows our real story but it's written in your eyes, in your energy. When you fake it, people know it.

You are who you are. Those compartments are deluding. If you hate your work and come home it will affect your relationship, even if you think you've compartmentalised it. There is no way, at a deep subconscious level that you can mask truth.

People know when we're lying, faking. They also know when we're inspired by life. People love to work with people who love their work. It's infectious.

I was in a bar in London and there was a young woman playing her guitar and singing. She was fantastic and people loved her. We sang along with her, and she made everyone in the whole pub smile. I bought her CD before I left to go home and as soon as I got home put it on to listen to it.

It was awful. What was the difference? It wasn't the singer, or the songs. What was different was that in the Pub she was just connecting with people, she loved her singing and the music was infectious. But the CD was her attempt to impress and because of that alone, I just didn't enjoy the feeling.

We're all performers. We're all leaders singing in Pubs or businesses or families. We need to remember, the more we love life: the more we'll affect others in a great way. No words need be spoken.

# Walk with a Quite Mind

A balanced, centred mind thinks clearly. I am sure you've had those perfect days where your thinking is so perfect, there's clarity, there's calm, you handle everything that comes your way, and people seem to respond in kind. I am also sure that you've had the opposite too, where you just want to curl up in a ball and go home. The difference is not the moon or the staff or the client. The difference between a great day at work and a bad day is your state of mind.

Learning how to bring Nature into your office will bring your mind to a calm, balanced, happy state whenever you choose.

When I lived in India a Ringpoche (reborn enlightened person) stayed as a houseguest. It was Christmas, and we hosted lunch for our mates. It was a great day; everyone bought food, Indian sweets and Chai and we just sat around eating and singing. One of the group played his guitar and one song we loved him to play was Imagine by John Lennon.

When all the singing stopped, and we sort of prepared to clean up, Ringpoche asked Peter if he could try the guitar. He'd never seen or touched a guitar but he'd watched Peter play and unbeknown to us, memorized the finger movements. Like some sort of magic movie; Ringpoche picked up the guitar and just played Imagine, he sang the words, and played the guitar so beautifully we all flooded with tears, we cried at the feeling, the deep beauty of his song. It was enlightenment in a guitar. Pure genius.

We're all Ringpoches in some form; we all have moments where we tap our genius. The question we must ask, in order to live our real potential, is how do we do it more often. This is the key, the new age of business.

Behind all the wanting, behind all the models of right way and wrong way, you sit in pure genius with an untrammelled mind capable of amazing insight and creativity. All it needs is for you to unlearn your habits of emotion that block it.

This is the gift of a quiet mind.

# Walk in Harmony

Emotional reactions, anger, and violent outburst were part of the old management paradigm. The new paradigm involves learning how to avoid reaction, and stay centred even when we're challenged.

One of the greatest books written on the power of the Human mind is Viktor Frankl's 1946 book 'Man's Search for Meaning'. It chronicles his experiences as a concentration camp inmate and describes his psychotherapeutic method of healing. It's an astonishing book, and totally worth ordering from your bookshop. One client of mine ordered it in lots of 100 to give to everyone he met.

Taking back the power of your mind, means being willing to change your thoughts. As Frankl advocates, when we identify with anything that can be taken away, we are vulnerable. And the deepest truths are neither thoughts nor beliefs.

I have been involved with thousands of peace loving people who refuse to bend their thoughts, they get stiff in their mind, they become brittle and run from violence to find isolation and peace. This is not peace; it is a really harsh way to live, a very bitter place because all the peace is built on the premise of hate. Hate for violence. That's no peace at all.

The enlightened ones who have walked this earth might have spent time in caves in order to find their path, but they rarely stayed there. They came to work. They put on their business clothes so they didn't frighten people, they turned up on time and they worked very hard as poorly paid teachers. Their mission was to create a great future for people, to give with kindness and to share their abundance. This is meditation in real life. The greatest of all.

We take this awareness to work and work itself becomes a meditation on the move, a mobile meditation of care, compassion, kindness and love.

## Walk your Truth

Mobile meditation begins with the most basic of self-mastery skills, the ability to be happy without things. This means that even if the Sun doesn't shine tomorrow, or the eggs are not cooked the way you like, or the effort you put in is to no avail you can translate that failure into a wonderful blessing. Nature dictates that there are two sides to everything. Harmony with Nature means knowing that in everything there is a wonderful opportunity to celebrate the moment. To feel rich, blessed and gifted.

Mobile meditation does not immunize you from pain and sadness because these things are real, natural and healthy. Instead you learn to celebrate the experience of sadness without sinking your ship every time it happens. You learn to smile and say, "Man, I feel sad today." Honest emotional awareness is vital but taking yourself too seriously is a big mistake. You have to hold your centre no matter what happens; yet, you can't become stoic and unfeeling. It's like absolute freedom to feel, but with the realization that it's only a movie.

The fastest way to bring your mind into harmony, and therefore be at your best at work is simply by offering gratitude to others. I know this sounds simplistic and it isn't the final step in mind control but it is definitely the path between an emotional state of mind and your totally inspired state of mind. One extreme is self-absorbed; the other is kindness to others. It can happen even by giving people your undivided attention.

## Beware of the Human Bomb

Have you met people who are "all about peace and goodness," yet seem to be frustrated? They talk about world peace and kindness and goodness but you feel like they are a human bomb ready to explode at a single drop of antagonism.

When we wrap our human fragility inside a philosophy we protect ourselves and it feels good. We then protect that bubble of isolation by wrapping a shell around it. We defend our philosophy in order to defend ourselves. Our vulnerability is now nicely wrapped in a shell and that shell is very rigid. We stand for world peace and we won't budge in a debate about it.

Inside that protective shell we have encased our vulnerability and with that protection of vulnerability we have accidently encased so much more that is valuable and inseparable from vulnerability. We've encased our free spirit, our joy, our open-mindedness and most significant of all, our ability to be loved.

This is the human bomb, advocating philosophy about saving this and protecting that, and making the world a better place while inside, there's a defensive war going on. A protective stance against all things bad, hurtful or cruel. This person remains single even when they are in a relationship, they remain protected. They really cannot turn up in life except say, in meditations, with animals that are harmless or people that are in pain.

# Walk with Consciousness

I did a conference where the theme was "honouring diversity." I asked the audience, "who believes we should honour diversity?" 100% put their hands in the air. Then I asked, "who believes that we should honour those people who don't honour diversity, and who judge others by race?" Zero show of hands.

So, when people say, "I honour diversity," they don't really mean they honour diversity, It means they honour those who think like them. It's a narrow band of acceptance isn't it? The diversity doesn't include those who are bad or naughty, but who made those rules?" Those rules were made by people who don't honour diversity.

It's hard to honour diversity really because then the pilot of the planes that smashed into the World Trade Center have the same right to be honoured as the saint who helps orphans in Nepal. It's just not what we mean when we say, "Diversity." We mean, we honour, some things as long as they are, "acceptable." An Israeli might honour diversity but do they honour the terrorist? Of course not. That's ridiculous.

There's a smarter language. A language that is not so prone to self determined definitions of who deserves honouring and who doesn't.

That alternative is consciousness. You can honour different consciousness without claiming to condone it. You can see low consciousness and you can see high consciousness and just label it. And as a new Leader, wanting to respect people and yet needing to remain competitive in your field, consciousness is the key to it.

The lower a person's consciousness the more management they need. So, people of really low consciousness might still be the smartest and best performers in an organisation, but they'll need significantly different management than someone of high consciousness who has a lesser job. This is a significant swing from the old paradigm that generally assumes that the higher a person is in rank in an organisation, the less supervision they need.

This is a real revolution in human resource management.

# Walk with Choice

People have a consciousness. This consciousness reflects their mind-set. Consciousness is neither good nor bad: it's higher or lower.

People of lower consciousness might hold extremely high positions in society. They might be very wealthy. Very successful. People of lower consciousness might be very spiritual or religious. There's no boundary that determines the aspiration or achievement of a person based on their consciousness. Consciousness is a measure, a pure measure of a person's motive.

You will have to be realistic. If you have an organisation with many people who are desperate or of low consciousness it will be very difficult to create a fast culture.

This is not criticism, it is respect for people's choices and it can save huge amounts of time, energy and frustration. If you expect people to respond to training or encouragement when their personal circumstances or believe systems hold them locked into a lower consciousness mind set then you will be wasting your time.

Whole communities of people sustain a generic consciousness and so it can be nearly impossible for you as a leader to impact their life choices simply by intervention at work.

This is very much the case when we deal with youth who come from troubled homes. Any training that does not address the environment and belief systems that exist in their home life will fail.

Another example of resistance to consciousness change comes from the unwillingness for some people to forget history. In one company I worked with, the leadership was having huge struggle to get change implemented because people had experienced a very negative breakdown in the company strategy some years before and were reluctant to forget and give trust to the new leaders. In other words their consciousness was stuck in the past. In this case we out placed about 50% of the team in order to trigger a new culture and consciousness.

# Low Consciousness

What is a thought? Ultimately the best answer to that question is, "a musical note."

Thoughts come from our head. The process of thinking is extremely complex but the process is not identical in every person's head. People not only think different thoughts, they think them in different ways. The process and the outcome is different. And this is where consciousness comes from.

In every head, even while it's sound asleep, there are pre-existing thoughts sitting there. We call these memories, but there's more. There are beliefs, experiences, ideas and a whole bunch of other stuff called expectations, hopes and desires. If we burn our hand on the stove, that creates a memory, and in future, we don't have to put our hand on the stove to experience the pain that tells us, "that's hot." We know it, because we believe it to be fact.

So, everyone's head is filled with this stuff. It's filled with information that in a sense saves each person from repeating painful experiences and helps them to repeat good ones. So, if someone said, "stick your hand on that hot plate," you'd probably use a fingertip to test it first. Your head is conditioned to help you get more nice experiences and avoid the painful ones. Now your 6 senses bring information to your head, you see, hear, feel, taste, smell the world around you and your head splits all that into good news or bad news. The bad news we avoid or reject, and the good news we attract or accept. This is the lower consciousness mind and everyone has it.

The important observation here is that everyone has it. We all have a part of our brain dedicated to lower consciousness. This is the human ego and it is dedicated to getting more good stuff and rejecting more bad stuff. It's quite emotional, it reacts to the environment through the senses, it is based on a set of preconceived beliefs that have either been experienced, like the hand on the stove, or driven into the mind by education, religion, socialisation, parenting or fear.

# Higher Consciousness

As people evolve their ways, they tap deeper and deeper levels of their Innerwealth. The more we evolve the less we resist change, so, as people evolve they become less fundamental and more flexible.

When people feel small inside they become resistant to change. They are generally defensive, seductive and desperate. They get emotional quickly or remain stubborn when things really do need to change. When people have a low sense of their Innerwealth they act with fear, so, even good ideas get rejected.

Innerwealth might not be the only mechanism to make money, but it certainly has a lot to do with keeping it. Some wealthy people who have a low sense of their Innerwealth act like they are poor.

Organisations shrink to the Innerwealth of the leaders. So, a person with a low sense of their Innerwealth might be acting out of desperation even if there is no need for it.

Low consciousness also leads to self-sabotage. People who don't feel worthy of abundance always draw their life and as many people around themselves as possible, down to that level.

Evolving an organisation is really focussed on keeping people focussed on a work paradigm that builds consciousness. By doing this, people expand their possibilities at work, and at home too.

To raise the consciousness of other people you firstly need their permission. You will be surprised at how comfortable people are being in the consciousness that they have created for themselves. The main reason is that it is safe for them.

Given that you have permission to coach individuals to a higher consciousness approach you have to consider all seven areas of their life. Any area of their life that has a 'got to' involved will need to be addressed. For example, if they have financial struggles and they have 'got to' pay bills out of desperation you will need to coach them up so that they save money and have more cushion between their income and their outgoings.

# High vs. Low

So what is higher consciousness? First, you need to understand that higher consciousness is not the absence of lower consciousness. We can't live without the lower consciousness, otherwise we'd need to burn our hand every time to see if the stove is hot.

Higher consciousness is the moving on from the lower consciousness as the only mechanism of response to the world.

So, higher consciousness is a forced divorce from the more natural way of thinking in a react - respond world.

There's a great quote by Danforth and it goes, "The person at the top of the mountain did not fall there." Higher consciousness is the same. The person using higher consciousness thought did not fall into it. Higher consciousness is a deliberate decision to consider more than auto conditioned response to the world, our senses and the thoughts that underpin our reactions to life.

Putting it in a nutshell. Higher consciousness is the deliberate choice to NOT respond, validate or react to EMOTION.

What is an emotion? It's a good without a bad, a right without a wrong, it's a pleasure without a pain, it's an upper without a downer, it's a win without a loss, it's an attraction without a repulsion, it's an acceptance without a rejection, it's a rich without a poor, it's a peace without a war. Emotion comes from half and the lower the consciousness the great is that separation. Lower consciousness is emotion based on half information. Like in the case of the stove burn. There was information, pain, there was no pleasure, we reacted, and hold that information as truth forever. Stove hot - burn bad - stay away. This is emotion at its most fundamental level.

But what if we hold those same emotions about people, places, things, words, ideas, thoughts and expectations and they are wrong? What if the REAL world out there and our emotional world are completely different? Then if we hold onto lower consciousness we might be safe, but we're in a sort of self imposed prison aren't we? So higher consciousness means we are aware of two worlds. Ours and the other one. Our world is in halves. The other world is in balance.

# More Consciousness

So, there are two consciousness levels? High and Low?

There are seven consciousness levels corresponding to seven different parts of the human mind. Each area of our brain can think different thoughts. People often only use the Lowest, and therefore get stuck in lower consciousness. That does not mean they are dumb, bad, stupid, or untalented. No, they are genius just like you. But what it does mean, is that they have no peace.

A mind that is functioning in lower consciousness is always responding to information that it computes in half story. So, things are either really bad, or really good. Or really right or really wrong. This is the emotional fundamental part of the mind and it's perfect if we are in danger of attack or threat by a Dinosaur. If we are in a war zone and we don't think with lower consciousness we'll be shot. But if we are in a war zone, it's probably because we think with lower consciousness that caused it. Catch 22.

Lower consciousness is always looking for half. Right or wrong, good or bad, better or worse. So, it has a very important function in our life in discerning safe or not safe. However, it's also extremely stubborn and resistant to change. Righteousness is the most resistant force on earth, it has caused every war, is underneath all domestic violence, is responsible for all human illness including depression and mental breakdown (bi polar etc.)

Lower consciousness is very important for people in danger: it triggers adrenaline, puts the body on red alert, places the mind in high wired states of readiness. It drains blood from digestion and other more long term functions and places it wherever the body thinks it will need it.

The irony is, that a person in lower consciousness can be sitting on the 50th floor of the most prestigious apartment building in the world, sipping Crystal champaign, surrounded by wonderful friends, with money dripping out of their pocket without a care in the world and still be on red alert. This person would be very difficult to lead and would probably end up as an entrepreneur.

# Using the Differences

As a leader looking for success it is wise to know the people you are leading. This way, you don't become deluded by philosophies that encourage you to treat everyone the same. Different consciousness need different management. This is compassionate leadership.

To simplify the seven levels of consciousness, I suggest you just use four categories of consciousness. They pretty much capture the essence of it. Those four categories are:

Black - Unconscious

Red - Lower Consciousness

Yellow - Middle Consciousness

Green - Higher Consciousness

Each of these states of consciousness has its benefits and drawbacks. So, it is quite common in an organisation to find all four states of consciousness and if they are in the appropriate jobs, then there's a great structural FIT.

However, if you need your organisation to be responsive to strategy, to change on a dime, then the black and the red levels of consciousness will be a problem. They resist.

I don't want to sound repetitive here, but I feel the need to repeat that there is no right or wrong when it comes to consciousness. There're just benefits and drawbacks to each level. I'm going to share those in the next pages so that you, as a leader, don't start loading the wrong expectations on the wrong people.

There is another important caveat on this leadership awareness and that is to know the difference between what a person might say and what they do. In other words, consciousness is not knowledge. People can be really, really, knowledgeable, they can tell you all about their higher awareness, but knowledge is nothing if it isn't applied. People can know heaps yet they might live none of it. That's important.

# Black Consciousness

There is a state of anxiety and fear that renders a person inactive. It's a state of overwhelm, too much information, too much emotional drama and the mind goes to glug. There's neither the instinct to run nor the wisdom not to. This is the black level and we can call it unconscious, depression, bipolar, and in extremes, schizophrenia.

When a person enters the realms of the unconscious, they are lost to action. It's a state many spiritual seekers accidentally stumble into and think it's bliss or enlightenment. Really it's a black hole.

A black hole is a place from which people find it hard to emerge, even with encouragement. They are depressed or disconnected to reality. In an organisation such a person is like a vacuum to the light, they suck the fuel from anyone who comes near.

Compassion is a valuable way, however, as a leader we are also responsible to the shareholders, the rest of the team and the clients. So, a person in a black consciousness might need to be isolated from all that. Anti depressants and deep psychological therapies might be needed because there is a possibility of self-destruction.

Black consciousness is not only infectious to the whole organisation, it is self-destructive. People in this state of mind can be quite negative toward themselves and others. It's a state that we need to avoid in ourselves as well as being vigilant about it at work.

To get out of this black consciousness people do all manner of tricks. They grab onto all sorts of systems to get out of the pain. They get angry, right, take drugs, smoke more, drink more and basically self destruct.

As a leader you will need to identify this state of mind as quickly as possible. It is not only self-destructive but can be destructive to the organisation and the culture.

# Red Consciousness

Red consciousness (Mini Me) is low consciousness. This is a state of mind very close to bi-polar. The individual is high one minute and withdrawn the next. Here people become quite deluded, believing in their own infallibility and sometimes taking extreme risks.

In less extreme Red Consciousness, the individual is highly emotional, prone to burst of temper, sadness, tears and joy - often in the same day. This consciousness is often the consciousness of artists and highly excitable creative people.

Red consciousness is also the old mindset of the sports personality or the sales agent. Highly volatile, determined and infatuated with the highs of life. This person will do anything to stay on an upper. Except change.

On the positive side this is a highly responsive, alert state of mind. Quite often hyperactive people get massive amounts of creative and clever work done in very short periods of time. The downside is the exhaustion, depression and burnout they suffer after it.

Leading highly emotional people who are in Red Consciousness is like managing an army. Your leadership has to be clear, directive and with strongly boundaries. If not, the emotion rules and the organisation will become led by pockets of emotions. Remembering that emotion looks for support to sustain itself and so, left unchecked emotion will seek out people with similar emotions.

Red Consciousness is on alert. It's the fight-flight mechanism of the human mind on alert looking for things to run toward, and things to run away from. It is rarely relaxed and therefore is often run down, exhausted, confused and leads to poor health.

No amount of balance will balance the mind in Red Alert Consciousness. Whether it is at home or at work, or on holiday. Recuperation periods and activities rarely last until that individual gets out the door. The immediately spring back into reaction and emotion.

# Yellow Consciousness

This is the perfect state of consciousness at work. It is neither unconscious nor deluded. In fact it is ambivalent.

You might be surprised that I use the word ambivalent to define a great state of mind, but ambivalent is, without doubt the most powerful place you can sustain. Here's why...

Anything you can't see the balance in runs you. Now, if you see the balance in something you can take it or leave it. Like a new car or a new relationship. If you can say, I can take it or leave it, this doesn't sound romantic or enthusiastic, but what it does mean is that you have the power.

Now, having the power is an interesting state of mind. It means if the world goes left, that's ok. If the world goes right, that's ok. You see, emotional enthusiasm is short lived and passion is for children. A person who is ambivalent is ready to act, ready to do what it takes. In the weirdest turn of events you can actually find that ambivalence and unconditional love, are one in the same.

Great thoughts come from a clear mind. That clarity is ambivalence. It means the work in front of you is neither pushing you away or sucking you in. You're the master of the work, not it the master of you.

When we speak of an open heart we speak of ambivalence. It's a state of readiness. Prepared to do what it takes, here in the moment. Not infatuated with the future, or the past. Rational, logical, calculated yet not retentive in thought. There can be no emotion in an ambivalent mind. It is neither for, nor against. This is the ultimate sport star, the best and most perfect leader, the individual who is doing what they love long term. (Sometimes mistaken for un-involved)

Try it. Instead of wanting to be right, better, good at, improved, better than, or anything comparative, just be ambivalent. Right in the middle, just do what you do. Detach from it. Do a letter with the awareness of ambivalence and read it through. See if there is clarity, honesty, integrity and you in it. The odds are, it's going to be written in half the time with twice the truth.

# Green Consciousness

There's a truck rushing at on you. The business is going bust. Your health is going to ruin. If you are in black consciousness you go down with the ship. If you are in red consciousness you have a panic attack and get emotional, if you have yellow consciousness you sit and work out a solution. If you are in green consciousness you don't give a damn.

Green consciousness (Maxi Me) is like the captain of the Titanic, "full speed ahead, she'll be right, the universe will look after us. Ooops, oh, goodness what's that big white thing?"

Green consciousness is perfect for the beach walk, the ashram, the temple, the monastery, the Church, the Synagogue. Green consciousness is perfect for making love or painting that Mona Lisa, or designing the next Opera House. Green consciousness is perfect when you are on stage and about to hit that absolute highest note of your career. Yes, there's a state of mind way beyond yellow consciousness: it's divine, sublime, fine and in time, but if you are crossing the road and you are in that state of mind, you'll miss the pavement, slip on the banana skin, bump your head, bang your nose, stub your toe. You'll also sabotage your relationship, screw with your finances and make dumb decisions. It's not the right state to live in unless you are a monk or some sort of cave dwelling enlightened one.

Green consciousness is where amazing decisions and great creativity can be birthed but once that thought is birthed, you'd better consider another headspace or the baby will fall to earth.

Inspiration is a magnificent achievement. To stay in that green consciousness you'll need a very safe environment because if your nervous system perceives any danger, you'll find yourself back in red consciousness in a flash.

Any person who turns up for work in green consciousness is a sitting duck. Their gift if fantastic and their creative genius will be extraordinary. Commercialising that gift, paying the bills, managing a life or a relationship would however, be a total disaster.

# Walk the True Path

In the old paradigm of business, people had a fixed set of duties to be carried out and these stretched a person's competence across a wide range of what were called "Responsibilities." It didn't much matter what potency each of these responsibilities had; they were simply the way an organisation lumped the duties together in order to get the job done.

The problem with that old way is that we're not using each person's potential. Before we get an ego, we have a constitution. This is a fixed, unchangeable biological disposition toward certain ways of working and leading. There are five constitutions corresponding to the five basic elements that make up the world: Earth, Water, Fire, Air and Ether.

All people have all elements. However, we have different quantities of each. Some people have more earth, some more air, some more fire, etc. So all people can do all jobs. The only questions are: for how long and at what cost?

In Nature a tree is a tree. A fish is a fish. They don't have the gift of a free thinking mind like we humans; so, fish swim and trees grow branches. Nature evolves them both by challenging them. Pollution, chain saws, bugs, and fishermen; you name it and Nature is evolving it. But people have a mind and that mind is coached to say, "I can do anything." If this were a tree it would be the equivalent of saying, "I can run." Nature built every human body for a specific function, and this is more a determinant of your style in life than any other single factor.

The key here is sustainability. If a fire person does water work they could be in hospital with a heart attack within 6 months. Or if an air person does earth work, they could even contemplate taking their own life. And depression is so common when water people get fire jobs.

This horses for courses work responsibility strategy is so important for work - life balance because if you don't know yourself, and you do the wrong constitution work, you'll be exhausted just by trying hard. Be who you are born to be. Honour your constitution before you put the ego on top.

# Understanding the Elements 1

Everybody is some combination of all elements but one of them dominates usually.

The diagnostic presented here is not complete, just a short grab.

First, you'll need to break an old habit, which is to think about how you do things and then work out your constitution from that. This is a big error based on psychological profiling. We say, "I pick my nose, therefore I'm a nose picker." That's not true.

Your constitution is based on your physical body. Nothing else. If you can just focus on that one thing, you'll get to see what you are built for, rather than the style you prefer. Our preferred style is based on too many variables to go into it here, but to summarise, we call it the Ego personality. Not a great measure of your truth.

Better to choose the top two that describe you and call them first and second nature.

**Earth**

Earth predominant people are: Heavy frame, strong boned, solid muscles.

**Water**

Water predominant People are: Soft flesh, heavy bones, rounded shape.

**Fire**

Fire predominant people are: Strong build, good muscle, average height.

**Air**

Air predominant people are small and thin boned.

**Ether**

Ether predominant people are tall and thin.

# Understanding the Elements 2

If you are an earth predominant constitution you are build for the heavy load. You are going to excel at building things, managing things, sustaining them and control. A very rational mind combines with the capacity to hold onto things makes you very resistant to spontaneous change and therefore an extremely reliable leader.

If you are a water predominant constitution you are built for caring. Your leadership will have a strong human ingredient: protecting, caring, nurturing others. Like the front row of a rugby scrum you'll put your own life on the line in the interests of caring for others.

If you are a fire predominant constitution you are built for change. New start ups, new business, new markets, new products, new people. If you are a fire leader you'll be great at starting new ventures, but please hand over the reins to earth or water people once those projects are up and running. Your passion for change usually sabotages long term stability.

If you are air, you are the multi tasker. You'd rather take a bite from everyone else's sandwich than to eat a whole one. You have a powerful creative mind, it can't be happy with just one project, one business or one idea. You need diversity and a finger in every pie. If you are an air predominant leader you'll thrive in high-pressure multi skill roles that require a lot of creative judgement.

If you are ether predominant, you are the visionary. Sir Edmund Hillary was ether predominant. He found the first route up the highest mountain in the world. Others had tried but he saw the vision of the future. Ether leaders are highly visionary, they lead with promises of the future and they are excellent delegators. They really enjoy and need support in bringing the dreams to reality. (Tensing Norgay climbed in partnership with Hillary to the first summit).

# Managing Earth

- Black State: Stiff, frozen joints, inflexible, strict, stubborn.
- Red State: Rude, short, brisk, cold, callous, resistant, closed minded, demanding.
- Yellow State: Stability, real, grounded, routine, methodical, reliable.
- Green state: Integrity, leader, wise, trust, pure, strong as an ox.

**Moving from Black to Red**

Do your share, perform as expected, do things their way, follow their routine. Be on time. Create earthy spaces with solid timber furniture, earthy colours. Feed them protein rich diet, saturated fats, baking, grilling, roasting, frying.

**Moving from Red to Yellow**

Provide a fixed routine, keep conversation on the facts, conform to their expectations. Focus on integrity, trust, truth. Be real, avoid philosophy or dreams.

**Moving from Yellow to Green**

Play some traditional music or something they like from the past. Look at old memorabilia, recall the past, think of old friends, provide safety.

**Moving down from Green to Yellow to Red to Black**

Emotional, changeable, out of control, things happening too fast, guess work, philosophy, half done jobs, broken promises, mistrust, unpredictable process. Process orientation not outcome clear focus.

# Managing Water

- Black State: Hopelessness, unmotivated, laziness, low metabolism, clogged.
- Red State: Sluggish, weight gain, procrastinate, slow, greed, clingy, attached, retention,
- Yellow State: Care, support romance, bond, coordination, attachment.
- Green State: Nurture, love, connection.

**Moving from Black to Red**

Reveal how you care about things, show how you feel, share. Be gentle. Use spaces with round corners, soft cushions, crystals. Provide food with oils, sugars, carbohydrates, boiling, steaming.

**Moving from Red to Yellow**

Help them to feel calm, peaceful and wanted. Encourage them to sit in a bath, or get a massage. Spaces with water features, food and drinks. Tell them it was extremely touching. Be clear and process orientated.

**Moving from Yellow to Green**

Be sentimental, talk about healing and kindness, compassion. Spaces need to have watery shades of blues and greens.

**Moving down from Green to Yellow to Red to Black**

Stiff structure, heavy pressure, changeability. Inhuman circumstances, outcome focussed. Things over people.

# Managing Fire

- Black State: Abuse, violent, criticism, acidity, joint problems, stones.
- Red State: Anger, change, frustration, judgment, passion, reactive
- Yellow State: Marketing, motivating, analysis, negotiation, power, intensity.
- Green State: Innovation, strategy, start-ups, inspired, power, energy.

### Moving from Black to Red

Provide strong colours, sharp corners, speed, bright lighting. Play romantic, courage songs. Plenty of exercise, action, application, interaction.

### Moving from Red to Yellow

Help them by being warm, precise, clear, forceful and sharp. Use illustrative phrases and talk about holidays, retirement, relaxation. Use the latest technology, and possibility for promotion. They like to win competitive situations.

### Moving from Yellow to Green

High intensity, discipline, beyond ego, Zen, focussed.

### Moving down from Green to Yellow to Red to Black

Rigid structure, flighty routine, being late, excess – (alcohol, drugs), uncertainty, loss, humiliation.

# Managing Air

- Black State: Stuck, hypersensitive, breakdown, self-abuse, physical aches, illness, panic attacks.
- Red State; Overwhelmed, anxiety, control, nervous, forceful, rigid, irrational.
- Yellow State: Multimedia, communication, variety, co-ordination, reliable, multi task expert.
- Green State: Inspiration, creativity, insight, wisdom, movement, dance.

### Moving from Black to Red

Soft mind, variety, re-assurances, curious things, colour patterns on walls and floor, light music, play, fun, open.

### Moving from Red to Yellow

Stimulate curiosity, joyful surprises, provide variety. Surround with stripes, patterns, bright colours. Emphasise relaxation, requesting, asking, searching, walks, eating regularly and light, deep breathing. Creative work, art.

### Moving from Yellow to Green

Nurturing, recovery, stillness, kindness to self, not too many changes. Mind control, nerve control, power breathing, face exercises, silence, stillness. Dance.

### Moving down from Green to Yellow to Red to Black

Disappointment, break expectations, rigidity, controlling, bland, predictable, repetitive, mundane, artless, lack creativity. Not fun.

# Managing Ether

- Black State: Depletion, delusion, self destructive.
- Red State: Memory loss, vague, confused, anxiety, fear.
- Yellow State: Wisdom, creativity, openness visionary, entrepreneur, ideas.
- Green State: Philosophy, new thinking, planning and advisory.

**Moving Ether from Black to Red**

Create open space, large windows and doors, skylights, calming music. Be open and accepting. Try to calm them and build up their self-confidence without words. Don't feed them heavy foods, raw, salads are best. Silence is their best friend.

**Moving Ether from Red to Yellow**

Use words like: the whole picture, philosophy, charity, meditation, humanitarian. Help them with goal setting, more focus, routine and schedule. Calm them with reassurance, peace of mind about their issues about the future. No aggression.

**Moving Ether from Yellow to Green**

Music: Subliminal, low volume, classical instrumental. Calming meditations, quiet space, open, white.

**Moving down from Green to Yellow to Red to Black**

Stiff structure, extreme emotions, heavy pressure, changeability, insecurity. Trying to push them into structure and rigid frames.

# Helicopter View - Work on it not in it

Whether you are an organisation of one or one million, you need to take a helicopter approach to your organisation. What this means is that you need to work on your organisation, not in it.

When I take a Leader to Nepal trekking, they usually start the walk with lots of questions about their organisation in their mind. They're challenged because they are still in the organisation. By the time they reach a few altitude gains, and start looking over the expanse of the Himalayas, they move to working on their issues, rather than be in them.

Even our language changes when we work on something at arms length. We might begin talking about my job, my organisation, my issues but when we have this helicopter view, we talk about that job, that organisation, those issues. This separation, the ability to observe from a greater height is one of the most important secrets of any leader.

We can't manage things we're in. We are actually part of the problem. When a close friend asked me to help with change in their business I willingly volunteered my time. I'd met most of the staff and they knew me quite well and because of this, gaining an objective viewpoint on the organisation was even more difficult than I expected. I'd become part of the system that I needed to fix.

Taking a helicopter view is often difficult. When our mind is messed up or we're having some difficulty at home, it's nearly impossible to step back in clarity. That's why we need a daily routine that includes some alone time. We need alone time in order to step back from everything and just observe.

A helicopter view is important in all the areas of our life. So, that stepping back experience on a daily basis can benefit our health, relationship and social world as well as our career.

This is a very important part of good leadership and self-management at work.

# Helicopter 1. A Leader's Questions

- Is the strategy for the future clear?
- Are the strategy and the vision compatible?
- Is the leadership model focussed on moderation or desperation?
- Is the strategy for the future backed by the right structure?
- Does that structure have clear financial resource modelling?
- Does the structure have adequate human resources?
- Does the company have a fall back plan?
- Do people trust the leadership?
- What is the history of leadership and has this tarnished confidence?
- Do people feel secure in their belief in the future?
- Are there factions of yesterday holding things back?
- What behaviour have people adopted in order to deal with reality?
- Are there people who need to leave but can't?
- What are clients saying?
- What is the market saying?
- Is quality improving or declining?
- Is profitability on a long term rise or short term?
- Is there cash from turnover or investment?
- Are these people willing to change and grow - seriously?
- Is there a good spread of ages in the organisation?
- Is there a healthy spread of male and female energy?
- Is there an openness to diversity, conflict and different ideas?
- Are people acting with integrity?
- Is there addiction to substitutes (read later in book)?
- Is there an objective measurement process for resource planning?
- Does the structural plan include the right human components?
- Is there a plan for helping people evolve?
- Do people know the key resource capacity of each job?
- Is the structure clear?
- Is leadership willing to support and challenge people?
- Does the cultural map reflect the future?
- Do people know what competencies they need to develop?
- Do people understand the benchmarks for success?
- Do people understand the cultural demands of the strategy?

# Helicopter 2. A Leader's Questions

- Have the cultural demands of strategy and structure been mapped?
- What program is in place to grow the culture with the strategy?
- What plan is in place to evolve leadership with strategy?
- Can the existing culture cope with the demands of the future?
- What changes need to begin now to cope with the future?
- Are people thankful for the dynamics of their work?
- Is there any blame game in the culture?
- What pace do people work at?
- Are there some core culture blockers in the group?
- Are your people in high demand from other companies?
- Could you replace people with more skilled or are they great?
- Is there an addiction to long term employment?
- Are friends, family, relatives employed who are under the radar?
- Is there a discipline or carefree approach to self-management?
- How are people handling stress?
- Is there a lot of emotional rhetoric?
- Is productivity creative and good or declining?
- Are people innovating?
- Are people getting more done in less time?
- Is happy one of the words you would use to describe the culture?
- Is there uncertainty at any level?
- Do people believe in the product?
- Is there a feedback system for people to monitor their growth?
- Is human development tailored to the individual or group?
- Do individuals have a personal plan for their career?
- Are they stretched, challenged, provoked and questioned?
- Would you use the word - Intense - in your culture list?
- How many people hold themselves accountable for growth?
- Is there any fundamentalist mindset - moral high ground?
- How, in general, are people's home lives?
- How many staff would think, "I've got to go to work today?"
- How many people in your organisation say, "Should" a lot?
- How many people in your organisation say, "I love my job?"
- How many people in your organisation say, "I love my company?"

# New Leadership - Summary

Times have changed. Leaders have changed and people have changed. An adaptation is required in order to recognise the extent and impact of that change.

A leader needs a fast changing culture. If strategy can change fast, then so must culture. This is the leader's limit. If the greatest leader on earth is faced with an organisation that won't change with him or her, then, we can say that leader will fail.

A leader is only as market adept as the culture of the organisation will allow. This ability of a culture to shift with leadership is totally conditional on the consciousness of those individuals within the culture.

So, the power for change is with the individual. What this means, is that a leader might have to honour people's free will and their choice not to change and adapt, by out placing them, or in more straightforward language, fire them.

The new leader needs to take a holistic approach to the human resource management of their culture. We have seen that culture change and consciousness are one in the same topic and consciousness is not limited to skill, capability, capacity, education or training. It is the mindset or disposition of the individual. This is the New Leadership.

# Chapter 4.
# Fast Culture
# Evolving People

In the whole dynamic of Organisational Management if the culture doesn't grow, nothing grows. All the dysfunction of organisational conflict comes back to human beings, unwilling to change their ways. FIT means people must grow at the same pace as strategy. And in some cases, that's instantaneous.

# What You Need

Building a fast culture depends on a few important things. They include:

1. The willingness of the Individual to Evolve

2. The skills of the individual to evolve

3. The awareness of the need (if it ain't broke don't fix it.)

4. The trust in the future

In an evolving culture we're trying to keep the organisation FIT. We're aware of the marriage between strategy, structure and culture and we want this relationship to remain healthy.

A culture that can't adapt is a huge problem. So, we need a very clear awareness of where we are right now from a cultural perspective, (see the Culture Audit in this Chapter) and we need to know where we're going (see the culture change process later in this Chapter) - then, we need people who are willing and able to make the shift, if any is required.

Evolution is a way of thinking that is adaptable and continually looking for opportunity for growth. Each and every incident is an opportunity, a guide post telling people to look at improving, refining the process, whatever it is. If a surgeon is doing open-heart surgery and comes to a difficulty, they report it to the research team and they come up with a faster and better process. Well, that's how corporate fast cultures are built. Innovation and new process, even at a personal level.

If the surgeon gets sore legs from standing for hours, or an aching back or loses concentration they report it, and research is done so that the surgeon is not distracted from their focus. Well, that's how people evolve. They find challenges; they look for ways to evolve so that there's a good focus. The key is to work on both the effect of the problem and the cause. If we don't work on the cause, we don't evolve, we just eliminate the issue for a while.

# Change Must Have a Benefit

When I ask people to change, grow or evolve the first question they ask is, "Why?" In other words, "what's in it for me?"

People don't resist change, they fear it. They fear discomfort and confrontation. So, when we ask a group of people to make a change, we'd better have some good reasons for it.

Once, causing change came by threat. It was do it or go - but those times are mostly gone. Now, there is a far greater need for respect. And trade unions have stepped in to protect groups of people from the "increase productivity or lose your job" syndrome that ran corporations a few years back. Yes, times have changed and this is what we're dealing with in organisational culture change.

Any organisation that does not evolve on a continuous scale is going to experience that evolution in the form of a shock (provided it is not a government funded not for profit organisation which operates under different rules). So, there's a massive benefit to people to evolve.

Shock change is "no choice" change. Whole industries have been wiped out because they didn't evolve. In Britain the steel and ship building industries resisted change at both strategy and cultural levels and disastrous consequences came to them. When unions, or governments make employment a priority over competitive performance there is going to be a massive backlash at a market performance level. It is far better to work hand in hand rather than in opposition.

When culture evolves and strategy evolves, people stay employed because the organisation is competitive. The market can expand as fast as the culture can expand. Then, the equation is not about staff reduction, it is about effective staff management. People who don't FIT would not be employed and replaced by those who do.

Respect for people, their beliefs and their choices is part of the changing management paradigm. However, that respect does not lead to more safety for employment. It leads to honesty. Great leadership cannot happen unless people are willing to evolve, and those who choose not to, can be respected, and asked to leave.

# Don't hide

When we hide from growth we attract disaster. It's a hell in a handbag because eventually growth catches up to us and we can't run. When I consult to small business owners all over the world, 90% of all their bad experiences come from lack of evolving management.

Exhaustion, bankruptcy, fatigue, marriage problems are all evidence of blockages in growth. This is particularly prevalent in entrepreneurial situations where individuals are not answerable to anyone except themselves (until the bank or tax department step in). We can think we're doing the right thing, even believe we're adapting, but many times people are just in delusion.

But there are early warning signs of blocked evolution because it drives people to substitutes. When we don't evolve, we become frustrated and there are four key substitutes for frustration:

- Food and Substance
- Greed
- Sexuality
- Spirituality

(More about this later in the book)

You will find all sorts of crazy behaviour linked to blocked evolution. Most of it becomes a social issue and few people realise the root cause of it. You'll find depression, obesity, harassment, bullying, sabotage, go slow, union powers, complaints, conflict, interdepartmental non co-operation, poor customer service, self righteousness, theft, self abuse, alcoholism, chronic fatigue and relationship heart breaks all tied to blocked evolution. So, there's a great benefit for dealing with it.

The conventional solution to this problem is stimulation. I've seen the largest consulting firm on earth get hoodwinked into transforming its office consulting space into a toy store filled with coloured balls, balloons and other game trinkets based on the "myth" that colour and crayons would keep some of the smartest business minds in the world stimulated. Stimulation is external, expensive and unsustainable; instead by evolving the culture at an individual level you are working from an internal motive, and this is sustainable.

## Working FIT - Tough love

We need to evolve. Some people don't want to. They are a leader's greatest nightmare. A leader cannot lead when people don't want to change, grow, evolve.

Evolution is Nature's single focus. We might admire the tree or the flower and this is splendid. But that flower will not exist in the future, it can't, it must evolve, just as you must. Anything that resists evolution gets consumed. People get ill, leaders get fired, employees get stressed, nations get attacked, tsunamis come, fires burn, businesses fail. All the result of a situation where evolution was being blocked.

Bringing the process of evolution to an organisation might best be referred to as 'Tough Love' because really, there's no choice and if we let the whole matter slip, in order to be nice and avoid confrontation, we only do more people harm.

Sometimes we avoid the 'Tough Love' approach because we like to be liked, or we think a few compromises here and there won't matter, but they do. Every time we let the culture slip behind the strategy, we sabotage jobs, the organisation and the responsibility as a leader.

Tough Love means everyone must grow. Those who resist get help but they cannot be carried into the future. Tough Love means short term pain for long term gain. Sometimes it's the unpleasant challenges that are the most important to deal with.

## Growth means 'everyone'

When even one individual resists the growth of a culture the whole organisation feels it.

Harmony comes when there's a zero tolerance to resistance. When people struggle with change this is human. When people question evolution this is also part of the process of growth. But when people just reject the idea of changing their behaviour, they take the whole company down.

In one company I was asked to consult with, the owner had employed some friends and family. Those individuals resisted evolution because it would have taken the organisation outside of their competence. So, they just held onto the past. I was asked to consult for change, but with these individuals with their foot on the brake there was no way it could happen.

What was even more fascinating about the situation was that the company had spent thousands of dollars on brand development, marketing, strategic planning and restructuring but the sacred cows of this firm, the family and friends had remained untouched.

Resistance to growth is different to conflict or stress. Unlike resistance, there's a constant growth from challenge and stress. When there's growth, the company gets more done in less time, and the result is always profitability. That profitability comes from productivity and can be shared, consumed or given back. The key is, that it happens daily. People are always looking for ways to improve their process. This is how an organisation evolves in harmony and avoids large hits of cash flow problems or commercial turmoil. The important things to avoid are complacency, comfort and peace.

# No Excuses

People can't be changed. They have to do that for themselves. So, real culture change is an individual responsibility. To change company culture faster you need to ensure that every person has the capacity to adapt to new circumstances. They need the tools to refine their work process and diagnostic skills to see where they are lagging behind.

That is a vital asset to share with staff. Now, if they don't want to learn then they don't want to evolve and if people don't want to evolve they are going to be a headache to themselves and the organisation.

The capacity to evolve work practices is the same within everyone but not everyone is willing to tap into it. People need the skills and knowledge of how to evolve. We need to teach people how to evolve daily, and this is why the Laws of Nature are so brilliant.

Getting more done in less time means each and every individual evolves their work practices. There's no end to the opportunities to work more harmoniously, more productively and with less energy.

When we evolve we learn how to deal with our existing circumstances better. We learn to do things better, faster and with less energy. So, although big changes might look and feel exciting, evolution means we do it one step at a time, less drama, more productive and certainly a faster approach.

Every time people evolve, they refine themselves and the work they do. They improve their process of life and make it more sophisticated. In evolution we move from clumsy, infatuated and all or nothing mentality to refined, accurate and productive mindsets.

This is the opposite to fundamentalism, which fights to be right, resists alternatives and is rooted in an all or nothing mindset.

# The Human Environment

There's no such thing as an office that doesn't want to change. There are, however, people who refuse and they hold everyone else back.

The environment for a group of inspired people can be rough and natural. They'll make the difference themselves. Inspired people make the space: they create the right space for themselves. They'll leave their mark too. When an inspired person enters a room they change it, just by their gratitude and presence. You can feel it.

Ritual is a vital key to create the right environment too because, in a business sense, it can include keeping regular time, leaving the office on time, not extending meetings and, can even go to the process of holding a meeting. In one company I was asked to do a culture audit on, they used a talking stick, an indigenous ritual to manage the respect in their meetings.

We can get strength from our rituals, when we are feeling messed up, or having a bad day. The key is to make sure your rituals serve two key functions. The first is to make you thankful for life. The second is to remind you of what is really, really important, a sense of real perspective.

Love and be thankful for what people do for you. Believe in their best potential, remember people become as they are treated. Set standards, don't drop them or compromise because compromise is the worst enemy of self-confidence.

Happiness, enthusiasm, good health and commitment are normal human qualities. People want to do a great day's work and they love being rewarded for it. But, when the energy goes out of it, or their heart is not in it, then substitutes are how people survive. They turn to food, sex, greed and spirituality to pull them or push them through life, as we mentioned earlier. Synthetic happiness is almost like an injection of good feelings and we could, make it unnecessary. Good feelings can be normal.

We must be committed to continual improvement, introduction of new techniques and evolve the way people work. It comes down to an individual and their willingness and skill to improve their space.

# Fast Culture - Finding nemo

In a whole ocean, there can be one special fish. That one special fish can be a delight or a man eater. It's reported that the chance of shark attack in the ocean is less than that of a car accident. But people still get bitten. When you do a culture audit you can be perceived as the shark, so be mindful.

A culture audit is often perceived as a witch-hunt. So, you need to be very clear up front when you do this. People can perceive that you're out to fire half the team, and then answers to questions, information will be diluted.

Do not survey staff when doing a culture audit. The answers to audit questions take three minutes and the best person to do it is independent of the company. Also, make sure who ever does your culture audit that they have business profit performance and client services as their motive for audit, otherwise, they'll be looking for HR issues. It's a sort of self fulfilling prophecy.

So, choose independent eyes. Make sure they have no HR agenda like selling training programs. Ask the right questions. Act on the results. All such culture audits start at the office of the CEO because they are usually a mini mirror to the organisation. Whatever is going on in that office is totally reflected throughout the organisation. So, you could save a lot of time just by going and talking to the CEO - that's where the FIT starts.

Find out how long people have been working in the organisation. If it is more than five years keep your eyes and ears open for comfort zones, superannuation motives, group think and power holds. People often gravitate to safety after 5 years.

When you hear the words, "that's the way we've always done it," or "oh, there's no need to check that out, it's perfect." Go onto red alert for culture blocks.

Please remember the objective of the Culture Audit as we provide it, is to prevent shock culture change. We're being proactive in planning growth and honouring the need for it at an individual level.

# Finding the Current Reality

If an organisation is FIT - then the signs will be so obvious. I've often walked around an organisation and in 10 minutes known that there's a great FIT. I've also felt the opposite in the lobby of a multi national corporation with thousands of employees. You can feel it in your bones. Trust that.

In a culture audit we're looking for the generic feel of the organisation. Is it in harmony or not. Now, in an organisation that honours diversity, you are always going to have bad eggs. One or two people who just go against the flow. A culture audit is not an extermination process. If you really want to honour diversity, you'll have to include the "challengers." The only question is, "How much power do they have over the whole momentum of the culture." Sometimes one single emotionally loud, cleverly versed individual can block a whole culture, and sometimes one single rational person can provide the perfect challenge. It's all a matter of influence.

Again, a culture audit comes from observation, not an anal retentive survey over the internet, or a psychological test to see if people are an NYPD Blue.... if you get my drift and if not, I'm talking about Meyer Briggs and the rest of those tests.

Where is your culture right now?

1. The Mood. What are people really saying?

2. The Intensity. What are people doing?

3. The Vision. What are their goals?

4. The Environment. Does the space inspire?

5. The Teamwork. What do people look like?

6. The Commitment. What pace are people working at?

7. Social Conscience. What are the humanitarian goals?

# Culture Audit 1. The Mood

Have you ever heard the expression, "You could cut the air with a knife?" or, at a concert, "The energy was amazing, everyone was up on their feet dancing." Have you ever sat next to a person who is taking anti depressants and felt their depression? Or have you been to a temple or church and just been overwhelmed by the love and peace of the place or the guru?

Mood goes deep, and we feel it, long before we even meet people. We pick up moods remotely, sometimes we are just picking up our own mood and blaming it on others, or the environment, so, mood detection is highly accurate but very prone to delusions.

When you do a mood audit within an organisation get your own mood out of the way first.

Start with the leader, his or her mood is going to have a huge impact. Then just walk around. Keep in mind that a great culture has support and challenge in it. Don't start looking for a kindergarten environment, don't project your own expectations onto the organisation, instead, let it affect you.

Certain areas are going to feel dead, no energy. Other areas are going to feel frenetic. You are not doing this to compare the culture mood to some pre existing expectation or model that you have in your brief case. No, you are doing a culture audit to observe, feel, experience the energy of the organisation. It takes a few minutes really. Sort of like sampling a wine, you don't have to drink the whole bottle to get the taste.

Always do a mood audit twice. Pick two different days of the week, to make sure you're in the right space yourself and, that you weren't turning up on a bad hair day for the organisation.

Mood is the most revealing element in culture change. It reveals the quality of leadership and the generic cultural norms within the organisation.

# Culture Audit 2. The Intensity

When an organisational culture is in FIT it's an intense space. People walk faster, laugh more, focus harder and, surprisingly, argue more.

Intensity is a fabulous sign of a well-led organisation. It's not sleepy or passive to work in a really great organisation. It's dynamic.

There is a vast difference between frenetic panic, emotional aggression and intensity. You need to know this in your own heart before you go into an organisation and start to judge the pace.

Intensity is not emotional. It's not noisy, rowdy behaviour or emotionally hyper active. Look at how people are sitting. Look at their offices and their posture. But most important look at the pace they walk because in a panic mania people run, in a dead forest, people crawl, and in an intense culture, people move with purpose.

Go shopping. There are people with money but no self worth who amble down the street as if time means nothing, just like their money. Then, there are people running, shouting, in a rush, they've got too much to do and not enough time, it's the height of unevolved living. Now, there're others. They know what they want and they have a time to get it. It's really about innerwealth.

What are you looking for in the Intensity Audit? You are looking for the energy of movement. The intent, the presence of people, and you are looking for the "culture blockers." Those people who've lost the run of the ball, a rock in a river, a concrete block under a tree root, a mountain of granite in the flow of the stream.

Intensity is a joy to work in. It's fun, focussed and productive. People leave the front door with more energy than when they arrived. Sloth, depression, emotional self-obsession are infectious. A person who is trying to become a Buddhist Monk might be a nice peaceful person to be around but in an intense organisational culture that's evolving toward perfection in productivity, time management and creative innovation they are about as useful as feathers on a crocodile.

# Culture Audit 3. The Vision

I promised myself when I began writing this book that I'd be honest with myself and you, the reader. And in this area of the culture audit I have to confess, it has been a very difficult job in my consulting.

I've run thousands of vision setting workshops, done vision quests, taken people to Nepal on Pure Vision Retreats but I haven't always been totally successful in this mission. I've found it harder than I expected to get people to let go of their paradigms of limitation in such short interventions.

I'd say my success rate is around 50% of all my clients that get a real, inspired, heart driven and higher consciousness vision. And it breaks my heart because without any doubt in my heart, it's the most important personal growth ingredient there is, because without a real heart driven honest vision, all that's left is emotional self-obsession.

If the only purpose people have in life is their own growth, then all life becomes is a drive to become more happy, more conscious, more enlightened, more self-obsessed and maybe this is great. However, from my side, that model is totally the opposite to the intent of Nature.

Until a person finds a purpose greater than themselves they are trapped in a self-obsessing paradigm of get more, want more, need more. It's a never satisfied mindset and in a corporate culture it's really destructive. Competition is healthy, but within a team, it's completely destructive.

In a Vision Audit, make sure you, the auditor is clear on your purpose in life and that you are content. Make sure your vision is clear, and that you have no hidden agenda to cause a commercial benefit to yourself in finding a conclusion.

Then, with your own agenda out of the way, ask people about their dreams, visions and hopes. Don't force it, if they have none, it's ok. If the leader has none, then it's not ok. What you are observing is the time frame people have. If their dreams, visions and hopes are for next week, then it's a desperate culture. If it's years then there's some evolution there. You just need to ask people what they want, when and at what cost?

# Culture Audit 4. The Environment

Some offices are decorated with trophies of company achievement. Some offices are decorated with the Golf Day Cup. Some offices are decorated with family photos and others have those motivational pictures with quotes on them. You can tell the culture of the organisation by those pictures and, you can change it using them too. This is the environment and it's one of the fastest - non shock - culture change mechanisms available to organisations: The environment.

There are firms with pictures of whales and elephants with quotes by long dead individuals on them on the walls. There're other firms that take photos of the staff and stick them on the walls. Another firm takes the photos from the last social night, usually the most drunken ones, and sticks them up to show what a great team they have. Other organisations invest in art and place that around to show how cultured they are.

There's fashion design, there's architectural design, there's accidental design and lastly, there're productive workplaces. Great cultures need a bit of all of it.

Fire people love red, and yellow, and green and blue. So long as it is bright and happy. Earth people love pastels, especially leather and wood colours. Air people love to work in any colour so long as it changes every few minutes and water people love cloth and carpet, anything that's soft and cuddly. Ether people love white. You see their favourite homes in magazines. White, with white, with a view of an ocean or something expansive.

There's no such thing as a generic human. Offices designed with one theme are relentlessly rejecting people. Offices where people don't invest in the organisation of their workspace lack innerwealth.

What's the feeling you get from the environment? Don't be judgemental, remember, it's not about money or facade. Does this space reflect what the organisation says it believes in with its products?

# Culture Audit 5. Teamwork

Great teams are built from great individuals. Individual people with individual goals, dreams and aspirations coming together for a common cause.

Individuals arrive in a team for their own cause. They have a clear personal focus, and they see the team game as being a great vehicle for that end. Loyalty, commitment and motivation come from the individual themselves. As long as they are getting their personal needs met, they'll play in the team.

People don't belong to an organisation. They belong to their family and themselves. They look to the organisation to exchange time for money. You can have the most belonging team but if you can't pay them, and their mortgage is at risk: good-bye.

Team spirit comes from a sense of belonging and that belonging has many dimensions. The main one, is certainty of the future. People commit to business, relationships, leaders, sports teams where they believe that the future is good for them.

When teamwork starts to fade, it is not always the individuals who have stopped co-operating. Very often it is because the future has become unclear. If people think their dreams, goals and ambitions will not be met in this team, they'll withdraw emotionally at least.

Great teamwork is revealed in clear communication, good feedback, positive attitude, confidence in the future, commitment by team members and trust in leadership. You can't buy it.

In the TEAM Audit look for process, workflow, eye contact, body posture and office layout. The signs include: respect, turning up on time, consideration, contribution and kindness.

# Culture Audit 6. The Commitment

Why am I here?

What use is this time I am spending?

Who benefits and is that really important?

Where am I going in the future?

What's the history and is that relevant?

What did the company do with that injured employee?

I audited an organisation recently where, everyt ime the management turned their back, people did home jobs. There was a real lack of commitment to the firm. When you do COMMITMENT Audit, look for the signs that people see their impact on the bottom line.

Sometimes people get the idea that the world owes them a living. They become accidentally lazy, and don't translate their behaviour to the long term survival of the business. This is very much the case in entrepreneurial organisations where the owner might be driving a very expensive car, and yet, paying people minimum wage.

Commitment is a precious cultural value and your measurement of this element of an organisation will tell you everything you need to know about the pace at which this culture can change.

Lack of commitment results in theft of time and assets. These are not always obvious in a culture audit but you'll get to know if they exist. Always look to leadership when commitment is vague.

# Culture Audit 7. Social Conscience

Social responsibility is, without doubt one of the key ingredients that makes people proud of their work. People require that companies have a connection to the world other than through product service delivery. Whether it's an orphanage or a humanitarian project of any description, people want to believe in the humanitarian conscience of their organisation.

In the SOCIAL CONSCIENCE Audit phase consider the bigger picture. How is this firm affecting the world, both with its products and services and with its profit sharing?

# Evolving People

Now you have a good insight as to how to measure the existing cultural norms of your organisation you might choose to consider what cultural norms will be required in the future and start the journey of getting there. If you wait until you need to change the culture, people or behaviour then its probably too late.

Proactive Culture Change - Doing it easy - Innerwealth

Culture change begins and ends at an individual level. People evolving their work practices automatically adapt to the demands of strategy, structure and culture. So, the effort in good healthy culture change is at an individual level.

For a culture that evolves there are two ingredients:

1. People have to be willing to change

2. People must have the skills to change

There are people who want to change and there are people who don't. And there are people who say they want to change, and think they are changing, but don't. So, willingness to change must be matched with the skills to do it authentically.

The key measure of evolution comes at an organic level: We simply ask, "Are we doing what we did yesterday, with less hastle, in less time, with greater quality?" Simple isn't it?

The skills to make those changes are a great asset for anyone to have both in their private life and at work. Refining our life process is a spectacular way of bringing more wealth, joy, happiness and health to our lives and those of others we are connected to.

Innerwealth Growth Process uses the Laws of Nature to help people change because they are grounded, apply to everything and can sort things from the smallest to the biggest issue.

# Tomorrow's Culture

So, we've talked about culture change and the three classical methods of achieving it. We now know that two methods involve culture shock and they are significantly painful to human Nature. One being a downsizing of the firm and the other being a market driven threat to safety. We've also seen that the former of those two is the most effective mechanism for fast takeover and performance turnaround and, the later is often done under extreme financial threat.

We've focussed on the third method and identified that historically this third method of culture change, training and development, has bred the first two: it's been too slow and during fast company change, is inadequate. So, our mission has been clear from the outset: to turn normal culture change into fast culture change. In fact, we want to make cultures evolve at the same rate as strategy, fast or slow, culture can keep up.

The key factor in this evolving culture is human development. We've argued that for a culture to move at the speed of strategy change, the power for change has to be at the grass roots level, in the hands of the individuals who make up the organisation.

We've also been mindful to respect those who are not wiling to be, do and think different, whether it be because of religious or philosophical reasons and we've invited those people to find other places to celebrate their resistance to change. If they resist here, in this fast change environment, they are going to pull the organisation, their team members and the customers down too. So, thanks and let's be clear, this culture change process is for those who aspire to aspire to aspire to evolve and grow at a healthy market rate.

We've seen that the universe evolves, trees evolve and specie evolve, Nature consumes anything that doesn't evolve builds a new one on top greater in consciousness (smarter) and less in number (more efficient).

We've also done a Culture Audit. That means you know where you are. That's important because if you don't know where you are, how will you know where to go?

# Planning Ahead

Now it's time to focus on where to go. What cultural values do you need as an individual and what cultural values does your organisation need as an entity to go where you need to go in the future? Think about an organisation just like one big person. That one individual has a past, present and a future. The past is gone, the present is already here, so, 100% of the effort of that person is really dedicated to making sure the future is what they want.

Desperate organisations are worried about tomorrow. Inspired organisations are not worried, but plan for the year, years ahead. I used to think, "where do I want to be in ten years, and how do I get there?" Now, with wisdom I'm more likely to ask, "Where do I want to be in ten years and what are the skills and talents that I need to develop to make it worth the wait?"

Our visions might be wonderful, accurate and competitive. Our dreams might be brilliant, smart and genius. Our purpose statement, mission statement and inspired concept might be absolutely unique: but if we don't have the meat and potatoes, the skills, talent and resources to get there in realistic time, then, well we're up the proverbial creek without a paddle.

So, in this chapter we want to know how? How are you going to get from where you are as a culture with human skills and abilities to where you want to be in some period in the future with new skills and abilities without the shock of a health scare, a bankruptcy or a domestic crash.

You see, your life and your organisation's life are running on the same laws, Nature's laws. If the tree wants to grow toward the sun, it better know how, and it better have a plan to hold those branches as it gets bigger, otherwise the council or a storm is going to lop the top off.

As a change agent let me say that when it comes to the human side of change there's a lot of room for people to blab blab about improvement without actually changing anything. Even in a culture where people want to evolve, they can do a lot of change but not really change. Knowledge that we can't implement is just intellect.

# Moving Forward

Cultures can really get stuck, especially when there's a long tradition of market dominance. Complacency is a poison in both business and personal management. This complacency makes the present a lot more comfortable than it should be. People start to hang onto the past because it's just too comfortable. I know it sounds crazy but challenge is a very vital part of good business and personal management.

One company I was asked to do consulting work with had changed everything over a ten-year period, or so they thought. They changed what they did. They changed who they worked with. They changed where they worked and they changed why they worked. But not once in their 10-year history had they change how they worked. The owner refused to change the process because he believed it was right. He employed the same team, and they behaved the same for ten years, like a traditional club or something, where old rules never change.

When it comes time to turn your organisation into a fast adapting entity, the first thing that's going to go is the old traditional rules. Those old traditions are great memories and important histories, but they are not sacred cows. You can touch them, and you must. Breaking through resistance has a lot to do with letting go the old traditions. It might be painful at first but it's far less painful than a lousy organisation that's stressful to work in, lacking FIT and in need of shock therapy.

To have a good fast changing business culture means that people work from their innerwealth; that really means, explore because your inner awareness is always growing, so, it means people don't get stuck in tradition, or even yesterday's ideas. That's the important thing about an evolving culture in a business, to keep the culture fresh, evolving even a little naive.

# ICCP Innerwealth Culture Change Process

Traditionally, organisational change at a cultural level nas not been a very rational science. HR departments and leaders can be really committed to keeping the skills of the organisation up to par, but that might not be good enough. Even throwing money at training and conferences might just be too generic. My estimate is more than half of the money spent on organisational training is wasted. The question is: Which half?

Here's how we've introduced the left brain into the right brain world of human development with the ICCP.

We create a retreat for stakeholders in an organisation. We either create or spell out the strategy for the next 12 months. We then group think the key questions for culture such as, "What key skills do people need to make this strategy happen." We come up with a list of 20 skills that almost guarantee the success of the strategy.

Try it now: On a spare sheet or the back page of this book list 20 human characteristics that would absolutely guarantee your success or increased success in business, your art or your home life. Choose one area at a time. Please try to avoid being philosophical, just list them in a practical way. For example:

- Creative
- Resilient
- Handles pressure well
- Able to change
- Good communicator

As long as you haven't become trapped in the altruism of nice guy and doing good, you'll have a real list in front of you of the "cultural" skills you need to get to make the success you want. Now, I know there are issues with your moral standards, and how you want to treat people along the way, but at least you now have a rational list of what you need to do to get what you want. It can't be easier. When you've learned those skills then apply the Innerwealth growth formula later in this book. And you'll be on track to the destiny you want.

# Innerwealth Culture Change Process

So, I hope you were able to create a list for yourself on the last page and prove that, if you take the fluff out, you can really quickly list the disciplines and skills you'll need to go where you want to go.

Well an organisation is just a big you. It has a direction, a set of resources, and it has skills. Those skills in the organisation are spread across many people and they collude in a culture. So, now, we're talking skills and cultural values that are essential to the organisation doing what it says, walking its talk.

When we do a culture change program we usually create a retreat to determine those characteristics amongst other things. But for now, just think it through yourself.

List the characteristics for the future culture and ask each and every individual in the organisation to rate themselves from 1 (lowest) to 10 (highest) on each of the twenty attributes. We then ask direct reports and peers to score that individual on each attribute. (We mediate where there's radical differences in scores which is very rare).

If the score is very high, we work to increase the use of that talent in the organisation. If it is low, we set up training for that specific characteristic.

# Chapter 5.
# Self Mastery At Work

When we search our heart for answers we are missing the point, the answer is irrelevant and self-solving. It is the question we should get right.

# Self Mastery at Work

We have a limited amount of time, a fixed amount of work, we have standards to reach and we get seriously punished if we don't hit those goals.

There's no use pretending that work is always fabulous. Sometimes we're flying and sometimes we're not. I'm here in this section of the book to make it more often than not.

There are a lot of things that affect our workday, month, year and life. Some of it has to do with luck. I made a fortune in one company I owned by being the worst manager I know. I lost a fortune in another one after doing so much analysis and study it was ridiculous. Yes, so, there's some luck involved but that doesn't excuse us from stuffing up our work life.

In the next chapter of this book I present a whole bunch of information on work - life balance. So, before we get too far into the personal mastery area, let me say that about 90% of the problems people have with their work come from a mess at home. Most people are not good at managing their lives, and it really does have a strong impact on their work and career. I think a good home life is fundamental to a good work life. So, personal mastery starts on a macro scale.

Then, we drill down in personal mastery to look at how people function in their day. It's extraordinary the opportunity we have to get more done in less time. Oh, yes, personal mastery at work is getting more done in less time. The whole idea is that we clean up all those things that cost us time and energy, refine the process.

Of course, this assumes that you have a life outside of work that you want to turn up for. I know that sounds a bit nasty, but, after 20 years of consulting to execs I promise, it isn't as weird as it sounds.

So, we're going to look at ways to improve the odds of your work life being a success. We're going to look at the way you think, breathe, eat, poop and talk. The key is to remember that personal mastery is a skill that is a way of work, not a conclusion or an end result. It's a way of always growing toward your potential.

# Your Real Genius

Einstein and most other great genius didn't feed off emotion. He claimed that it was the single greatest opponent to his research. He used a different science. The Laws of Nature. Yes, there have been thousands of people, who have used the Laws of Nature, to eliminate petty emotional highs in order to create inspired work. Einstein for example, immersed himself in his laboratory for days at a time, undisturbed, in order to sink down through his emotions, down into the well of his soul, into his inspiration. In that state he was completely emotionless.

There are others too, well documented people who prove the new paradigm of inspired work. Miro, Galileo, John Lennon, Elton John, Princess Di, Pavarotti, Bach, Beethoven, Mick Jagger, Gwyneth Paltrow, Sean Connery, Richard Branson, Bill Gates, Elvis all tapped or tap that same Einstein genius. Some knew why and how, others just stumbled into it and then came out into confusion. Some handled their genius because they understood it, some couldn't work out how it happened, and those were the ones who self-destructed.

Now, those people are pretty extraordinary, or are they? Maybe they're just role models of what is possible for anyone who chooses to live outside the emotional container that holds the mass consciousness. People who knew themselves tapped into astonishing genius. Gifted people. But I believe we're all gifted the only question is, do we put emotion before inspiration? If you put emotion before inspiration then there is a personal choice you are making and that's ok as long as you know it.

Balance exists everywhere in the universe, except in emotion. Balance exists in the stars, in molecules, in forests, in human health and it exists in the human mind. However, our sense can't think in balance. Our senses, for pleasure and pain, emotional senses can only measure one side at a time. So, all emotion comes from half thoughts.

Genius is beyond all that half thinking. In fact, when you tap your highest potential you aren't thinking at all. There has to be another word for it. You don't get tired, you forget time, you know things you have never learned. It's a miracle really.

# Evolve Your Work Style

When the pressure of work comes on, the most simple thing to do is expand your work hours. Sometimes it's even a corporate measure of how committed we are by 'putting in the hours," we are deemed to be showing our true colours. For many people, even after 30 years business experience, they are still, "putting in the hours," in order to get the job done. After thirty years they've only had one year of experience, thirty times. Their work practices haven't evolved, and they needed to. Time is not the best resource to handle increased workloads.

Instead, if we lock down on the time frame in which work has to be done, we birth a magnificent resource, which can be called evolution or innovation. This is the creative exploration of "how" we do things better and faster.

In my consulting practice, nothing is sacred; I question all the process "how" things are done. And if you could be a fly on the wall you'd hear the most extraordinary justifications on earth as to why the process shouldn't change. In the most part this resistance comes from the fear of losing some form of hierarchical control, and that can even mean their job. But we can't get stuck with process that doesn't evolve, to work in harmony with Nature everything must be open to refinement, everything evolves, especially work practices. The System must keep up with the strategy.

Here's how it works. Anything you do twice the same, automate. We need to systematise anything that can be systematised. We need to change the process of anything and everything we do to make it happen within the time that's fixed. Did you hear Parkinson's Law? Work expands to fill the time allotted to it. So, we fight the expanding time syndrome, you go home on time, every time, with all the work done.

It takes courage to turn the paradigm around. However, you need to see it as a real investment in your business life and your personal life. Get more done in less time and therefore the more competent you are the faster and better you do something. It means that the one who leaves the office last, and works the most hours, needs help to grow.

# Do It Once, Do It Right, Do It Mindfully

Multi tasking is another "presence killer." Doing two things at one is fine as long as one of those things is not important.

How can we be 100% focussed on what we're doing if our mind is split? In spiritual language "turning up" is referred to as mindfulness, but it simply means, "being present" and doing whatever it is you are doing, with 100% commitment.

When people talk about balance they are most often talking about time. And yet, if you examine their mindset within those time allocations you'd be shocked at how little value they place on the integrity of what they are doing.

Much of the skill of success is in the art of mindfulness. Doing one thing, doing it right and doing it now. To bring your mind and body into the one experience of life. The great actor knows how. The entrepreneur knows how. The spiritual sage knows how. People who achieve great things know how to bring their whole being into the moment and stay there.

Mindfulness is a habit. It starts with the way we place things. Never throwing things into place, we place them mindfully, carefully so that there's a respect for small or large objects. Mindfulness is also experienced in the way we eat. Mindful eating includes the way we chew, handle and consider our food.

Mindfulness also extends to our work-life balance. If we spread ourselves too thin in focus at work then we'll be thick with control and heaviness at home. Or, if we're not mindful at home, we'll become extremely insecure at work.

Mindfulness simply means we do one thing at a time. We concentrate on that one thing. When people go into Nature this is automatic, the environment causes it and there are few distractions. But in city life we can easily see something out the corner of our eye while we are talking and this means we are doing two things at once. We lose presence. So, mindfulness is a considered approach - especially in communication with others.

## Everyday Improvement

Everyday ask yourself these questions:

How can I do repetitive things in my day faster?

How can I do more of what I love in that extra time?

How can I turn up more?

How can I balance my emotions from yesterday?

How can I live more in the direction of my purpose in Life?

How can I be more authentic, and not put on an act?

How can I turn up more in communication?

What can I do what I do in less time?

How can I reduce waste in my time and life process?

# Prevention Is Better than Cure

My job is to help people solve problems and create solutions that last. The most remarkable thing in my job is the realization that people cause 90% of the problems they have.

90% of our stress is self-imposed and, in the same way we add hours to our keep fit program through poor lifestyle and bad eating habits. So much of what we do, is really undoing what we already did poorly.

We cause so much of our drama in life, and nearly all of it is completely unnecessary. By trying too hard, by following some life philosophy that doesn't work or because of some pre-existing belief pattern we cause nearly all our own problems.

For example: People with lung problems who still smoke. People with Gout who can't give up red wine or meat (both cause gout). One young lady who couldn't sustain a relationship for more than a few months before her boyfriends dumped her, couldn't, in her language, stop having sex on the first date. A businessman whose financial circumstances were always struggling but who kept sacking his accountant. And the couple who were so obsessed with pleasing their in-laws, they forgot to ask each other what they wanted for Christmas...

People who can't manage their emotion make twice the noise, seem to have twice the fun but make twice the work for themselves in everything they do. They also have twice the emotional pain that everyone has. So, loud, emotional and dramatic might be entertaining, but it's a lousy process to bring to any type of relationship that's meant to last.

Emotion is a choice that breeds plenty of highs, and as a consequence plenty of lows. That's unavoidable. So, you don't need to feel sorry for those who have emotional lows, they've already had the high, the upper and the wizz fizz. It's just balance that's all.

# Beyond Emotion

What causes people to become extremely unbalanced in their work –life is emotion. People who can't manage their emotions can't manage their business, or their life because they become vulnerable, unwise and act from uncertainty. They can easily mismanage business and they mismanage themselves.

In the long term – The pain of regret outweighs the pain of discipline.

Getting past emotion as a guide to anything in life, be it business, health or relationship is a really big step into wisdom and out of the drama. It is certainly at the heart of good business management and self-mastery.

To manage without emotion, you are going to need to find an alternative to conventional thinking. That's why the Laws of Nature are so important to learn. They put the wisdom back, where emotion has taken over.

Emotion can motivate us. Emotionally stimulated people work enthusiastically. Emotionally disgruntled people can become terrorists in the name of their emotional beliefs. Emotions are hard to separate from truth. An Olympic champion will tell you that there's no room for emotion in the final of their event, and the loser will say, "I just had too much emotion." It's the difference between the winner and the loser. One taps into their nerves, the other remains inspired.

Whenever we break discipline, commitment, focus and our dreams, emotion has overridden our real ambition. So, emotion is the short-term experience of life, and it's a very important experience of life. The key is, not to believe that your emotions are based on anything except half-truth. In other words, they are fictional interpretations of life. Our anger, our infatuation, our hunger, our desire, our jealousy are totally emotional, and therefore, valid experiences. They are however, totally deluded.

## Turning Up - Value Your Time

I wanted to learn Spanish. I talked about it and even bought the CD. I even learned one word here and there. The problem was I was busy and didn't have the time to do an hour a day. After a year, I still didn't have time. That's the problem for lots of people. They, like me, chunk things into all or nothing and don't do anything... So, I put the Spanish on my Ipod and I listened when I was waiting – I'm always early – and I listened when I was in the taxi. I just grabbed a bit here and there. So, I started to learn Spanish... Exercise is the same. People say, "Oh, I can't get to the Gym, so I can't exercise." But that's bad news. Sitting in your chair at work, with the inner core muscles tightened, breathing right, walking briskly instead of sexy, or stopping one stop before home and walking the rest. It's exercise and if you're not expecting to run the 100meters in the Olympics, then it's going to be these small things that'll make the world of difference. Chunk it down...

# Set Priorities - Lines in the sand

Your boss might ask you to do many jobs and some of them are within the scope of your job and some not. Your boss, if you are self-employed might be life itself but no matter who requests the use of your time, it is only you who can determine the value of it.

People can often accidently devalue your time. They can ask you to work on things that are not in their higher priorities, and therefore assume automatically that they are permitted to devalue yours. This is where you need to value your time.

The first thing to ask is, "What are my responsibilities." Then, with the measurable outcomes of your work all mapped out, you can ask, "What are the four highest priority tasks that will get me those outcomes?"

This is how you set priorities and all other duties must, in some clear way, link into those four highest priority tasks. For example, Robin came to me with serious financial issues. I asked her what her goals were, and then I asked for a run down on how she spent her working day. 99% of her productive time was spent on really low priority tasks. She was devaluing her time, and therefore she was being paid what she really thought she was worth.

When we work on low priority tasks we beat ourselves up. So, the boss might be happy that you spent all day trying to find something, but you'll go home internally angry. Your Innerwealth will be down, down, down on your private stock exchange. You'll be having a bear run, and when you get home, you'll be acting like a grizzly one.

I think this one small insight can explain most marriage failures and business failures. My observation of thousands of people is that we don't value our time well and we often work on low priority tasks. In a relationship, if your priority is intimacy and love, then a priority might be spending time alone together, romantic candles and walks in the park. But many couples, who want that, talk work, watch TV and play with the children to fill up their free time.

Set priorities and make this your religion.

# Put Your Heart into It - 100%

When our heart goes out of our work we become tired, frustrated and critical of ourselves. That's a really nasty situation to be in because if we lose our self-respect we lose the respect from others too.

The key here is to make your self-worth a condition of how you work rather than a condition on what you work on. Even if you don't have work right now, you can do something productive and creative. And even if that is not a very important task, you can do it with your heart and soul.

Have you noticed that where people have plenty of time, where there's low employment the space gets really messed up and there are usually a lot of babies around. When people feel lousy about their work life they lose respect for their inner self, and that reflects in their outer environment. The way people compensate is, sexuality.

A woman came home from work, it was 7.00pm and she was exhausted. She sat down on the lounge and put her head in her hands and began to sob. She felt awful and no one seemed to understand why. She'd seen all sorts of doctors and received all manner of advice, but she was exhausted all the same. A friend dropped over and invited her to come down the pub for a few drinks, and nothing seemed better than that offer. At the pub, they were sipping their beers and having a few jokes when the band started to play. It was an old 60's number and they both smiled at the familiarity with that good old music. After ten minutes or so they couldn't help it; they had to dance. Soon the dance floor was packed and some guys joined them. It was laughs and fun and at 3.00am the woman and her friend went home. What a great night. So, was she really tired? Exhausted? Or was she just beating herself up from boredom?

There's no balance program, holiday, yoga class, tennis club or affair that's going to put back into our lives what "a bad attitude at work" is taking out. My guess is that 90% of all doctors' visits are triggered by this one single piece of disharmony. When we don't work, or work for all the wrong reasons, tiredness and sickness become more frequent. And they get worse, until there's a chronic illness.

# No Compromise at Work

Jenny ran her own company and it was really successful. She travelled the world with her team and they were a formidable force. Clients loved dealing with them. It was a great business and everyone made money. Then, Jenny met a man and he started travelling with her and the team but his mindset was old school, and he wanted to assert himself in her life so, he started to change the work dynamics between the team and with the clients.

On many levels, Jenny's new man was right. I mean, her systems were a bit organic and her team had a lot of emotional struggles. But the clients loved them, they loved their work and there was profit growth. So, Jenny compromised her own style, her own values in order to do the "right thing." As a leader this also meant that she betrayed her team because she, as a leader, compromised her relationship with them based on the personal desire to please her new man.

Torn between wanting to please her new man and wanting to run her company, Jenny lost a lot of business and because of his methodology, he made the client relationships more formal so the organics went out. Jenny still provided great service but the clients didn't like dealing with her so her business shrunk badly.

People love working with authenticity. They don't want false fronts or highly efficient business operations, they want human beings that do their job with passion and of course, deliver what they promise. The process is very adaptable as long as the client enjoys it.

There's a masseuse in Australia who is an ex rugby player. He's the strongest man I ever met and he gives the most painful healing massages I've ever experienced but people line up for an appointment. He's fully booked. Why? Because he loves what he does, his work and his intent is to heal, no compromise.

Set your standards in the process of your work and don't compromise them. This means, that you work to a process that you enjoy and you defend it. This begins with the way you work.

# Control Your Mind

1. Sit still.
2. Hold extreme gratitude (thankfulness) in your heart.
3. Be free from emotional and physical pain.
4. Open your heart to whatever comes to your mind.
5. Feel the lightness and joy of life.
6. Have no emotional attachments for this time.
7. Be in silence where you cannot be interrupted, disturbed or distracted.
8. Focus your heart and mind on an object in front of you; just relax.
9. Surrender any expectations of an outcome.
10. Keep your spine straight.
11. Balance your breathing; inhale and exhale the same length of time and pressure.
12. Keep your eyes open at all times.
13. Any spontaneous thought, write it down, keep a pen nearby for notes.

# Respect - Deserving

Susan ran her own successful company but she was always in financial troubles of some sort. In her office people were abusive, they were disrespectful and there was compromised integrity everywhere. Susan came home everyday wired, sensitive and emotionally wrecked. Her willingness to compromise at work, destroyed her balance, and her home life just couldn't compensate.

As a leader you need respect. This respect can either be earned or demanded. At lower levels of human consciousness structure sets the hierarchy and therefore respect is a part of the process of business. At higher levels of consciousness people need to volunteer their respect.

This whole idea of respect begins with the self-belief that you deserve it. This is the foundation of respect. If you act like you deserve respect, then you've taken the first step. If you feel that you deserve respect, then that's the second step. But if your results show that you do what you promise, then, your respect is validated.

In the situation with Susan, her team did not show respect. This was because she was friends with some of her senior people and they didn't want to empower her over themselves. Also, Susan was reluctant to assert herself because these people were friends. This is a deep pollution in business dynamics.

The other reason that Susan's company struggled was because there were no standards of behaviour set company wide. Some of her team were allowed all sorts of liberty with standards and ethics, while others were told to toe the line. Double standards in an office or company are one of the worst compromises, and it always leads to personal drama.

# The Victim

Don't blame anyone for how you feel. Become absolutely bulletproof in your happiness and joy in the process of your work. It's infectious so it helps your business grow, plus, it keeps you really attractive to your partner because you feel worthy of their affection.

Remember, nobody does to you more than you do to yourself. If you feel ugly or out of integrity, or if you feel unproductive don't ask your partner to feel great about you. All they can offer is sympathy.

When we get into the victim mode we blame everything. We always have an excuse. Dave came to me with poor health, exhaustion, and tiredness. He reeled off 20 reasons, and gave 20 more names of people, naturopaths and doctors who had given diagnosis to help him distance himself from being the cause. Like, the air was bad, or the dust caused it.

I spoke to Dave harshly, "mate, if all these things cause all these problems, and all these things are outside your control, then what are you doing coming to me? I can't fix Sydney's air pollution or the dust in your carpet. While you are the victim of the circumstances, you are going to seek remedies."

He quickly recognised the issue and asked how to turn it around. "Simple, we find out why, on an emotional - psychological level is that you are having all these symptoms, we make you the cause of all the problems you have and we fix whatever it is in you that's causing them. Really simple stuff."

Dave was defensive, "But I am not the cause."

When I teach consulting techniques to my consultants one of the first things I share with them is when to know that you are going to fail. I teach them to recognise a "failed client," before the failure. I say to them, "don't take bad clients. It's corruption of your value, it's going to make the client angry and, it's putting commercial needs above your reputation. Your reputation is your greatest asset, don't compromise it. You can't help victims until they really want to be helped."

# Evolve

It's hard to do good if you don't feel good. Enthusiasm is a state of mind and the key to it is to approach everything we do with Nature as a guide. By immersing yourself in Nature, and using the Laws of Nature as a guide you can explore better ways to live and breathe, always evolving, healing and growing your life. A permanent balance.

Try to get things done in the least time, with the highest quality, with the least energy with the highest result. Refinement is Nature's way.

Incremental changes are far smarter than lumpy ones. Small things everyday can hardly be noticed but over time evolve us. It's like losing weight. Lose a gram a day, not a kilogram. Small steps are permanent steps.

You are mind, body and spirit – evolve yourself everyday by learning, exercise and meditations like prayer and ritual. Your work is strategy, structure and culture – evolve your work everyday by vision, process refinement and gratitude.

A tidy mind is a tidy desk

Posture affects productivity

Breaks are important but need to be efficient

Mornings are always more productive than evenings

Always line up meetings back to back on one day of the week

Invest in systems to do what can be automated

You can also evolve from errors. Every disaster has a silver lining. As a leader your job is to find it. Learn from mistakes. Learn from disasters. As a leader of anything, even the leader of yourself, learn from your circumstances and you can live without the anger and grief that comes from regret. If we can learn from a situation, then we are not afraid of it happening again.

# Chapter 6.
# Work-Life Balance

When I was young and free and my imagination had no limits, I dreamed of changing the world: as I grew older and wiser I discovered the world would not change, so I shortened my sights somewhat and decided to change my country, but it too seemed immovable. As I grew into my twilight years in one last desperate attempt I settled for changing only my family, those closest to me. But alas they would have none of it! And now I realize as I lie on my deathbed, if I had only changed myself first, then by example I might have changed my family. From then, by example, I might have changed my friends. From their aspirations and encouragement I would have then been able to better my country, and who knows, I might have even changed the world.

Inscribed on the tomb of an Anglican Bishop at Westminster Abbey.

# Mind Your Spirit

We have inside us all a spirit. It's a child about 3 years old and it loves life. It loves life and it brings joy. It's a light, a spark and if that spark goes out, well, we become adults.

Adults make money, own business, get married. But adults have no joy. They have things, like money and cars and partners and children. Adults have things but the joy and energy that comes with them, is a pure child like spirit.

When the spirit goes out, we go out. When the spirit goes out of work, we survive it. When the spirit goes out of a relationship we survive that too. There's nothing wrong with a spiritless relationship, or a spiritless job in fact it's normal. People find ways to live without the spirit of their inner child and they're OK, so let's not get into criticism here. Spirit is joy, and many people live fine without it.

However, there are some problems that come when the spirit goes out. Most of them are personal but all of them lead to social issues that governments, communities and families would love to fix. They are called the four substitutes and you'll read about them in more detail in this section of the book. When the joy and spirit goes out of something, then we substitute: Food (including alcohol and substance abuse): Greed (blind ambition): Sexuality (affairs and more): and, most surprisingly Religion and spirituality (escapism and righteousness).

When we lose the spirit of something like our work or relationship it is not a disaster. We can survive. But our health, wealth, joy and energy will drain away. The substitutes are trying to put back what Nature gives automatically. And there is no pill to replace the human spirit. I know this, because I've tried.

Everything is easy in retrospect, but now I can clearly see that during the early 80's my heart and soul went out of my work. To anyone who knew me, it wasn't obvious, except that I was drinking more alcohol, getting all spiritual, cheating on my wife and being a bastard in my work life. It's hard to believe that I could be so 'successful' in my work and family life yet be so corrupted. It was all a matter of smoke and mirrors, substitutes propping me up. But it didn't last long.

# Nature - A tough teacher

The problem with substitutes like: food, alcohol, affairs, greed and fanatic spiritual practices is that they end up taking more than they give. They are perfect short-term fillers when the real energy is gone, but they always have a cost. That cost is in the long-term.

When our spirit - energy - joy - goes out of our relationship, work, self or life, we're into the zone of self-sabotage, even if we don't know it. It's now 20 years since my catastrophe, and now, I can see that all the warning signs were staring me in the face. I was just too obsessed with survival to notice.

Those warning signs were Nature's guidance to me. "Chris, get your life together!" but my ears were shut, and frankly I felt like I was doing fine. I mean, a few glasses of scotch (sometimes four), an unlimited budget for boy's toys, my own business and therefore plenty of things to blame for my woes, and a fanatic attachment to spiritual yoga which made me feel - how do you say it - more pure than a snow drop. I had such a great system of denial going that not even my partner, family, friends, doctor or Yoga Guru noticed.

But Nature did and She's a tough teacher. She's not going to allow one single member of her whole family waste a life. Within 12 months, my business went sour, my marriage failed, my health went into recession and my bowels jammed up. My friends deserted me, my business partner bought me out, I had some sort of nervous breakdown and I needed therapy. From winner to total loser in 12 months, and no one was more surprised than me.

In Canada I am known as the Spiritual Pit bull. It's not because I'm bad or mean, it's because I want to help people get past that same denial that kept me from seeing that when my spirit went out of what I was doing, I was in a fight with Nature that I could never win. In Australia we have that expression, "She'll be right mate," and it will be but we need to be honest with ourselves. Sometimes it is better to be confronted by a professional who knows what they are doing and acts with compassion than it is to be hit over the head by nature with a 2 by 4 piece of wood. In other words proactive personal growth is better than experience.

# Avoid Compensation

It is very important that you avoid the trap of compensation. It pollutes one area of our life with the incomplete stuff from another. It usually results in messing up both. It's very common; in fact it's the norm rather than the exception. It stems from the fact that people don't know how to find harmony in their work or their relationship so, they try to compensate one with the other.

Compensation doesn't work. My observation around 90% of all work related productivity and management issues are really the result of compensation for disharmony at home. And, this might shock you, 90% of domestic struggles come from an attempt to compensate bad self-management practices at work.

When we try to balance something that we don't like with something that we do like, say a job we don't like with a relationship we do like we screw both of those up. We aren't present at work, so we're always making mistakes and forgetting things. We aren't present at home because we expect too much. Both suffer, and we'll often cry, "oh, I need a holiday because I am so out of balance" but really, no holiday is going to fix this, in fact if you hate your work and spend your holiday with your partner to try to recover, you'll probably blow your relationship as well.

Say you're really under pressure at work, what sort of home life are you going to want? You would want calm right? So, in seeking a balanced life, we often use our home life to compensate our work life. But it also works the other way too. Sometimes people go to work trying to compensate for a difficult home life.

If we can't walk through our front door happier than when we left in the morning then there's something wrong. If we come home complaining about being tired, then we are asking our partner to have a relationship with a second hand self. We're bringing home the crud and leaving all the good juice at work. This is really going to play one off against the other.

Avoid compensation: do right at home and at work. No compensations necessary.

# The Real Thing Please

When we are out of integrity to ourselves, following some compromised path and out of step with Nature, we use substitutes to survive.

Substitutes are like the rations soldiers carry in their backpack. They are there for emergencies. You wouldn't want to live with them permanently. But people do.

Substitutes are temporary energy replacement mechanisms that we use when our heart goes out. Our heart is like the natural fire of life and when we are healthy, doing work we like and with love in our relationship, we really don't need substitutes. There's just no appetite for them.

However, given that in our busy lives we can so easily lose touch with our true Nature we can observe our real life balance quality by our attraction to substitutes.

There are many ailments that we can trace back to the concept of a substitute that has become addictive. So, being aware of your attraction to substitutes can help you heal your health and stay true to your natural way. However, I think an even greater reason to stay aware of your attraction to substitutes is that this reveals the real quality of your life.

As our quality of life decreases, we increase the use of substitutes as replacement fuel. If our health, our work or our relationship are operating at a substandard level, then we will see this in our groping for substitutes.

For me, this has been one of the most powerful awareness of my whole spiritual path. What it has shown me is when I am running away from challenge and when I am avoiding something. I'm not hard on myself for taking substitutes, I just don't want it to become a permanent habit. I aspire to life and love and great work as my fuel, not substitutes.

# Substitute 1. Food and substance

Food, alcohol, substance, sugar, pharmaceuticals, herbs and remedies are the first line of replacement when our heart goes out of life. They are the most immediate temporary fix and can provide instant fake energy sources. Because they are so easily used, they are the most addictive and usually the subtlest.

We reach for and over consume those things that make us feel better – fast. When we're in denial or in a place that really hurts our heart, we feed our soul with food. It's a temporary substitute for good life, and love, and inspiration. Obesity is really a wonderful way to witness the food substitute in action.

Even obsessive paranoia about health foods, organics and natural products can be a form of substitution for real happiness. The individual who has lost the joy of life can often seek it in a health food shop, self-obsessing. It's a form of compensation that is like massaging your toe to get rid of a headache. Feels great – solves nothing.

Alcohol is a food. Taken in moderation it is meant to be healthy. But taken as a substitute it is the prime choice for those with depressions, lost vision, hopelessness and inner turmoil. Personal dishonesty is masked by the substitution of alcohol into our diet.

It is the sugar in most foods and alcohol that forms the core of our main socially acceptable substitute. It stimulates mental and physical activity and makes a person feel totally happy for a short stint. This is the drug of choice for the average person in our society who has lost their heart and it is highly addictive, toxic in excess and leads to around 99% of all medical ailments that plague our communities.

Excess consumption of food, alcohol or substance is an important sign that an individual is out of harmony with Nature. Rather than let it progress, or even worry about it, we are far wiser to seek out the source of the issue. Why has their heart gone out of their life?

# Substitute 2. Greed

When we feel poor we want to fix it. For many people this inner poverty drives an outer desire for wealth. This is how a substitute works. It deals with an issue in one area of life and patches it up with another.

This is a quite normal dynamic that motivates a lot of people. However, external wealth never fills the internal poverty issue. So, no matter how much a person who has an internal poverty accumulates they'll still want more. It becomes an obsession and the more time that passes, and the more wealth they accumulate, the poorer they seem to feel inside.

At some point the substitute of outer wealth has to be removed so that the real issue of inner poverty can be replaced by innerwealth.

If we choose to deal with our real issues then we can be proactive about it and there's a healthy growth. However, if we don't deal with those issues in real time, then Nature seems to sabotage the function of the substitute. In this case, a person might totally lose their outerwealth because it was blocking them from dealing with their innerwealth.

Greed is the last line of defence when we are trying to fight against Nature. People sense that they are vulnerable and start panicking. This is greed, and there develops an obsessive - compulsive attachment to money, people, places and things. It's the equivalent to hanging onto the cliff face with your fingernails.

It is in this awareness that many teachers get messed up, blaming money and our desire for it for our social issues. This is not true. The use of money and the desperate struggle to hold onto it as a substitute for innerwealth, this is the real issue that drives anti social behaviour.

# Substitute 3. Sexuality

Much of our sexual needs come from a desire to compensate something deep. A man who loses his real passion for life might have an affair. A woman who loses her love of life or herself might fall in lust with a new partner. People change their sexual preferences, flirt, and cross all manner of boundary in sexual expression in order to replace the heart they lost in life. They are really compensating for something that is a natural part of living a healthy life.

We flirt and play with energy in an attempt to dig our way out of heartbreaks and emotional pits. Using sex as a substitute for real life heart and soul is a quick fix that doesn't last. And it causes so much loss of real life force too.

In many spiritual teachings they advocate the idea of abstinence from sex. This is not because sex is considered bad, it is simply because sexuality is a great hiding place, a pure and available substitute for real spirit and love. So, by abstaining, they feel that people will become more honest.

I don't find this to be the case at all. There are many horny people walking around denying their sexuality in a physical way but using it in all other sorts of ways. So, blocking out the physical act of sex doesn't really mean people aren't being sexual, it just forces it into different forms.

Nature will not turn a blind eye to the use of sexuality as a substitute. She closes in on our nervous system, our feelings of goodness, eventually, if sexuality is used as a substitute in any form, Nature unravels it and people eventually face their real life challenges. It is just a matter of time.

If our heart goes out of life we often seek sexual approval. In this way we might use sexuality at a time when we feel the worst about ourselves, instead of the other way around.

## Substitute 4. Spirituality

When the heart and soul goes out of life, people often turn to spirituality as a substitute for it. Spirituality often gives people what they lost in a marriage breakup or a personal drama because it, like sugar, sex and greed, feels better than loss.

But spirituality is a substitute. The spiritual individual is a natural person who finds their spirituality in everyday life, rather than an Ashram, cult, Guru, "New Age" speaker, born again fundamentalism or meditation classes. Such things are invented to help people when they lose life, and therefore they are temporary substitutes.

The one who loves their home and their family is the spiritual speaker. There is no need to add what is already natural. We only seek spiritual release from life if we lost the love for it. Compensation by spirituality is a wonderful nurturance for the damaged life, but it is no answer. Nature needs no analysis, it's already perfect, and just like we are: already spiritual.

We substitute for real heart and soul in life by putting on robes and flashing our ego all over the world, "hey, look at me, I'm a Buddhist." This substitution is great, it helps the fallen stand up again, but it's just another label and it eventually peels off.

When we attach to spirituality for what Nature gives us naturally, we put on a mask that is no different to sugar or cocaine. A prop to help us through a time, but eventually, we need to let it go. It is not a healthy attachment. Life is the best drug to take and a well managed life is a heart filled soul driven experience. Who needs spirituality then? We're as spiritual as we could ask for.

# Wisdom

There is no one-way to live life. Wisdom is more about knowing the options than it is about knowing one way. The Laws of Nature are an option, a good option because they don't come pre-packaged in a "should do this, and shouldn't do that philosophy."

There are many different ways to do everything, so, this is more about exploration than it is about nominating one particular pathway. These are guidelines only and with that in mind you might find some great insight to improve your quality of work-life balance.

Please remember that work-life balance starts in your head. If you think out of balance you are going to need rebalancing. So, if you think in balance then there's no real need for rebalance. You just love your work and love your life and put time boundaries on things so, there's a sense of discipline.

It's my personal opinion that we are guided in our life. We are guided by Nature, our intuition, our emotions, our vision and our soul. So, often there are conflicting directions to take. Each one has its own gift and really, at the end of the day, they all end up in the same place: we die.

When it comes to work-life balance we can save ourselves a huge amount of time by not stuffing things up in the first place. I've experienced the wisdom of my soul, and the wiz bang of my emotions and I can vouch for the gifts in both. The main difference is the amount of drama we create, and therefore have to repair.

I think the most important thing to know here is that we are actually quite transparent. What I mean is that our secret life, and our deeper thoughts affect our life much more than we think. This is both a positive and a negative. When we are filled with joy and happiness it's infectious, and when we're feeling uncertain or insecure we cause ourselves continuous drama. I don't believe anyone sets out to self-sabotage but we do it regularly. So, these hints that come in the next pages are designed to help you prevent problems before they need to be fixed. Balance things before they need rebalancing. Don't Bring It Home.

## A Master In the Art of Living

**Draws no sharp distinction between
Their work and their play
Their labour and their leisure
Their minds and their bodies
Their education or their recreation
They hardly know which is which.
They simply pursue their vision
Of excellence
Through whatever
They are doing and leave
Others to determine
Whether they are working or playing.
To themselves, it always seems
As if they are doing both.**

**Christopher Walker**

# Manage your Work Life

David was a successful entrepreneur, his business life was busy, he travelled a lot and had his share of ups and downs. Independent and wealthy, his only real issue was his relationship was turning to dust.

Jenny's company was cash short and was on the edge of going broke. Jenny had challenges at work but none of those compared to the pressure she was under in her personal life.

Michael worked for a large multinational. His heart was not in his job but his mortgage and his financial commitments to his holidays in Bermuda gave him little choice but to stay in the job. His wife had recently revealed that she'd been having an affair.

Greta had a great job. She loved it and if only her teenage children would get their life together she'd be totally happy. A single mum, Greta had been dealing with the police over her son's problems.

Rose and Peter each ran small businesses. Peter worked two jobs to bring in his share of the money to keep their savings plan on target. Rose was committed to buying a home soon, her business, a high profile fashion company was doing well. Peter on the other hand had diversified to follow his life dream. Their relationship was on the rocks.

Jane and Mike had three children. Their business was doing fine and their children were doing fine. They were doing fine with everything. Until Mike had an affair. Trust was broken and now another family was about to break up.

Susan had a breast cancer. She'd done everything she could to be healthy and yet, here she was facing one of life's greatest challenges.

All these people came to me for advice on their personal life issues but all of their problems started with the way they work. They thought their relationship or their health was more resilient than it was and subsequently they didn't protect their most precious gift. Protecting your relationship, family and personal life is the beginning of healthy work-life balance. Let's explore how...

# Protect Your Relationship 1

A person who comes to their relationship after a great day's work will be a really interesting partner and probably a great lover. They'll be relaxed, feeling abundant, and quite inspired about life. So, although I write here about relationship, I do believe 90% of the essence of great relationships starts with our work life. If we can refine our work life, be effective, do something we're passionate about, we'll be magnetic and wonderful as a partner.

The pressures of everyday life and business are making relationships more and more difficult. Protecting your relationship, family and personal life from the ever increasing demands of work is a really important commitment. But this does not mean working less, achieving less or doing less. What it means is working smarter, not harder.

By working smarter, you do more in less time. You use technology where it saves repetition. You think before you act. By working smarter you automatically accept that certain human behaviours are normal and you don't get disturbed or take things too personally, instead you stay focussed and again, get more done in less time. Like a great actor who can do a scene in one take instead of 20, you become a working person who can do their job in "one take" rather than fluff around.

Relationships thrive, and survive when we have a good work life, and this is where a lot of energy needs to shift. As a society, we are putting a lot of pressure on our relationships because we still operate on the premise that longer hours means better productivity. It is like putting water in the fuel tank of your car and wondering why the car doesn't go well. Long hours, exhaustion and hard work do not make a better performance at work. Quite the opposite really.

These days partners and families expect and deserve a healthy, happy, enthusiastic person coming home from work. So do you come home from work and give kisses or take them? If you come home from work inspired, you'll be loaded with energy and want to give some. If you're managing your work life badly, you'll be coming home more like a Hoover Vacuum cleaner. Looking to your family for balance.

# Protect Your Relationship 2

When people die, very few of them wished they'd worked harder or longer hours. Their regrets are usually around family and loved ones. You see people think that their relationship is more resilient than it is. They overwork and break commitments or turn up tired and every one of those subtle compromises costs far more than people know. Compromise says to your partner, "You are not so important as... "

The relationship is the most vulnerable to bad balance. As I pointed out above, people think their relationship will handle all they throw at it, and they count this as a measure of the love they share. It's total rubbish. Love is respect, trust and many other things but it isn't the willingness to tolerate abuse.

- Don't come home late
- Don't come home tired
- Don't bring your work worries in the door
- Turn up for your partner inspired by your work life
- Give 100% to your work and it will send you home happy.
- Don't ask your partner to counterbalance your crappy day
- Keep your private life immune from work culture dynamics
- Don't think 5 days work - 2 days home life. It stinks.
- Don't take your partner for granted - they've got needs too.
- Don't bring your home life to work
- Come home more energized than when you left
- Give more than you get at home
- Setting these boundaries will force the evolution of process at work.

There is a great opportunity for all of us to grow. Refining the process of work, refining our human relations, refining our definition of productive work so that we don't pass on antiquated work practices and sabotage people's home life. We need to protect what we value, not by avoidance, but instead, by evolution.

# The Honeymoon that Lasts Forever

When I wrote and published my book Sacred Love - The honeymoon that lasts forever. People criticised me for being unrealistic. They claimed, "Real relationships can't live up to that." And for a long while I began to doubt what was and still is, my firm belief that the honeymoon can last forever.

To be attractive, you have to make others feel good in your presence.

If you are unhappy, then all your doing is trying to compensate, but it just won't work. My experience has been that happiness is a personal experience that you have before you go out into the world, and you carry it with you everywhere. That means you give happiness rather than need it.

When we go on the honeymoon, we're obsessed with making our partner feel great. This is because we feel really happy and just want to make our partner feel happy. There's no self - obsession in it at all.

Self-obsessing isn't really attractive on the honeymoon, and it's no more attractive when we get home. To stay in a great space and feel balanced we need to turn up happy. That means we need to be content with ourselves as we are. Content with our life and with the world around us. The complaining person who sees only the negative of the world, the environmental destruction and worries about the global warming, is actually polluting the world more than any corporation they might complain about. Turning up content means a good heart, an appreciation for life, just like it is.

Don't compromise your relationship. Hold each other strictly accountable for "turning up" happy, enthusiastic and just as committed as the first day you met. Hold each other accountable and don't make excuses. You can evolve your self-management practices to deal with increased work pressures. Hold your relationship absolutely sacred, and when you can't do that, at least admit it so your partner can make wise choices around it.

# Do Good - Feel Good - Treat others well

At work, there's no need to compromise yourself. Just take responsibility for everything that happens and don't give yourself justification for treating others badly. Begin with respect for everyone, whether they deserve it or not and carry it through to all your dealings with people. Keep your chin up at all times and, don't let your mood run your life. You have great power to affect your state of mind, and you can hold yourself accountable for the way you impact people.

I've put enough self-management tools in this book to make compromise a thing of the past. You can do the worst job with the toughest people in the most challenging circumstances, with a smile on your dial if you learn this gift. Try not to read it all and then "bring compromise" back with you, because then the power of creativity is lost, you might not have the energy to think up new ways to do old tricks. You must use the intensity of no compromise to treat people as you'd love to be treated. Use the energy to get more work done in less time. Avoid being the cause your own suffering.

In your relationship don't compromise. In relationship every compromise in the standards for your romance, your intimacy and turning up is a nail in the coffin of the relationship. It's a deep nail because it goes straight into your heart. There's no need to compromise. You have the skills right here in this book to turn up 100% in your relationship and at least, if you slip, to know it and warn your family in advance that you're too dumb to sort out your own mind. No excuse, none.

# Beyond Myths That Run People's Lives

Myths are wonderful tales and while we are able to label most stories and fairytales as myths, there's a whole bunch of stories and fairytales that we think are actually real. And because we don't label them myths we really get ourselves up the creek without a paddle. The ultimate damage comes when we start expecting the whole world to turn left when it really wants to go right.

We've all got a head full of ideas about how the world should work, could work, and might work.

There can be no peace in our heart while our pre-conditioned expectations are the foundation of our reality. So much of our imbalanced work life is caused by tensions that come from myths we call real. Stress is one such consequence where, people become tense because they feel threatened or questioned, when really, threatened and questioned are healthy signs of good communication. So, we end up doing communication training on how not to be a real person. The screw turns another notch.

It is by far the most important element of good stable inspired balance to learn how to see the two sides of every coin. To accept that our opinion is right, but so is everyone else's. We must, at all cost avoid getting trapped in the myths that run people, and their business and their relationships. If you can see beyond myth, you'll see harmony, and feel it, no matter what you are doing.

The key is to live with an open mind. The egoistic temptation is to be right, and therefore argue against anything that contradicts your ideology. But this is a disaster for the human spirit and for society. It's a disaster for our relationships and our business life. Being right never solved anything and it's the source of massive humanitarian abuse.

Global change begins inside your mind, and if you can just achieve this one discipline in your life, the idea of an open mind then you'll have a healthy openness to others.

An open mind is not a dumb mind. Simply it sees two sides to everything, just as Nature intended. There're two sides to a leaf, so, there's two sides to every person, and there's two sides to everything they do.

# Balancing your Life - Go with the flow

In Nepal when I take my groups up to Gokyo Re, The Sacred Lakes of the Himalayas. I teach clients how to walk with the mountain rather than against them. But those old competitive habits are hard to release. People try to achieve the summit rather than go with the flow.

Those mountains, like the structures of our business and societies have been around for a long time, so it's wiser to work with them, rather than compete against them. The Sherpa people of Nepal are a great example of this idea in action. Life can be difficult in the mountains, so, they've learned to go with the flow, rather than fight it.

The process of going with the flow is about appreciating the moment, enjoying each single step. Then, the most important place we can be is 'right here', and we value our temperament rather than the summit. We stay cool and generous, even when the going gets tough.

It is easy to let the emotions of exhaustion, fear and fatigue overwhelm us, so, I teach each person how to observe the beauty of the walk, no matter how challenged they feel. In this way, they go with the flow of the mountain, rather than set goals and try to beat it.

For work-life balance, this is a very important awareness. Balance comes primarily from the ability to "turn up" no matter what the circumstance. We learn to manage our mind and emotion so we go with the flow of life, rather than against it.

So, Nature's harmony comes to those who learn to go with the flow of life, rather than carve out chunks of it. It's a visionary process, no one is suggesting that we live aimlessly. The whole idea is to set the vision, the dream and then focus on the process. Like an Olympic Athlete, they want Gold Medals, but the more they focus on winning the Gold the less likely they are to achieve success. All they do is focus on the flow, be in the moment, enjoy the circumstance.

I don't think we can predict the future 100%. Life is going to present us with challenges and those challenges can either make or break us. For my suggestion: emulate Nature, adapt, stay on track, evolve.

# Turning Up

There is no greater compliment that you can give, than "turning-up" for someone. It means that you've dedicated this time to a communication with them. You've actually focussed on them for this time.

"Turning -up" really means that the only thing filling your mind for the few minutes you're with someone, is them. It's the opposite to self-obsession. We owe it to people to "turn-up."

When we "turn-up," people feel met. They feel respected and valued. And this alone makes the world of difference. Earlier this year, I went back stage to meet Carlos Santana after his sell out concert here in Sydney. He'd been playing on stage for nearly 3 hours, non stop, he came off stage, took a bottle of water and came into the meeting room. He was totally present with us, he'd fully left the stage, he wasn't puffing and huffing thinking about dinner or a rest, he was 100% present and the four of us spoke for nearly 40 minutes until his manager reminded him that 30 other people were waiting next door. He was the celebrity who had just played to 20,000 people and here he was talking charity and giving love and advice to four people he'd never met. So present, yet so humble.

Learning to relax into your true Nature must come from deep inside, a friendship with yourself that is perfectly natural, undistracted. It's all there already, nothing we need to do except to protect this beautiful innocence from our own ego. Our most natural state in life is ego free and open, fully present, "turning-up."

This "turning up" is a very high spiritual state. When I used to study sitting meditation we had to sit perfectly straight, eyes open and unblinking, body perfectly still and mind focussed on our breath. It was so intense, because we just had to learn to control our reflexes. We couldn't be distracted by our mind, emotions or our body. No matter what happened we remained in perfect presence. We were absolutely "turning up," right there in that microsecond of time and this is called being in the moment. Sometimes I'd drift off, distracted by an ache in my spine or some emotional tangent so the monk would wack me with a stick. I'd snap back into the moment and I'd be present again.

## The Spiritual Side

So those Zen retreats just teach us what we already know. There is really nothing to learn. Just stuff to unlearn. We have the habit of scratching every itch, talking about nothing, worrying about the weather. We have the idea that emotions are real, but when you sit in Zazen, you watch your emotions come and go. They are like clouds that came over and block the Sun, but, if I didn't react to them, then eventually those clouds blow away. The Sun, our happiness is always there, even if the emotional clouds block our awareness from time to time.

Doing what you love is a natural form of ZEN. When you love your work you're present with it. When you love your home life you're present with it. Have you ever gone shopping to a place that's boring to you and noticed how tired, or even ill you feel. That's lost presence. So, doing what you love and loving what you do is the real everyday art of being in your true Nature. And this is a critical key to life because if you hate your job, and want a happy relationship with yourself or someone else, then no spiritual ashram or guru or therapist on earth is going to get you where you want to go; there's no way you can force happiness for more than a few moments. That lack of love and the consequent lack of presence at work can't be 'balanced." If you hate your job or your home life, you are out of balance and nothing, not even a month in the Bahamas is going to resolve it.

The ultimate aim of all spiritual development is to stop wanting. To stop the pain that wanting creates, and the main way to achieve that is to learn how to be in the moment naturally. It's really a matter of letting go. Letting go the distractions that take you away from what is already yours. Sometimes we need a meditation cushion and a harsh stick to give us this awareness, but for some people, like artists, photographers, sports stars and performers, they know this experience already. It is their real life.

The key is the capacity to translate the skill from the stage to their home life. We might know how to kick a goal, but can we be present enough with our beloved to make them feel met? How can we achieve this while we're distracted by body, mind and emotional anxiety? The answer is we can't. Presence in this moment, "turning-up" now, is our truest Nature, our highest spiritual achievement.

# Stop Wanting - Be happy

When you "turn-up" it means you don't want to be anywhere else. That means you are 100% focussed in this very moment, nothing lingering from the past, nothing anticipated in the future. Can you imagine it?

To achieve this great state of mind you'll need to learn how to become content anytime you choose. Contentment means you are totally happy with life as it is. Nothing to fix, nothing to change, perfectly happy with things just the way they are. Of course, there are a few challenges you'll need to deal with. So let's explore them.

The greatest challenge you'll need to deal with is your wanting mind. Our wanting mind simply doesn't like wherever we are no matter how great it is. Wanting mind is always thinking, "gee, if only..." So, your wanting mind is never satisfied, totally unable to be content. You'll need to deal with this little bugger before you go any further on your journey with this great work.

When you stop wanting to be anywhere else, or do anything else with anyone else other than who you are with right now, you've arrived. There's no desire to improve it, change it or make it better. There's no interest in comparing it to last year or your plans for next year. It just is what it is, and you are thankful for it.

I hear people say, "I am where I am meant to be," and this is a great technique for accepting the present moment as the best moment. People are just waiting to feel your presence in this moment so, if you say, "I am where I am meant to be," and you really mean it, they'll really feel it.

Your partner, your work colleagues and your family are waiting for you to "turn-up" right here in the moment and be content with what you've got. But most people miss that chance to be around. Many people arrive in their mind or body, but don't really "turn up" because they can't switch off. The "if only" mind is running for some people 24/7 so, if you want to be felt, be appreciated, be attractive and give people the gift of your presence, best to stop wishing for what you haven't got.

## Prevention Before Cure

The best way to overcome a distraction is to prevent it before it happens. There are innumerable technologies for repairing life. But the best cure is always prevention. Going to the doctor after five years of bad posture and seeking a remedy for your back pain, is such a destructive process. Let's try to "turn-up" in a good way, and prevent the issues - like worry and emotional drama, before they happen.

If you examine the self-help industry and the health industry, you'll discover that 90% of all the problems people are dealing with, they caused. It is an extraordinary discovery to realise that we have not adapted to city life as fast or as well as we thought. Whole industries are established to repair what should not, in a healthy world, need repairing.

Our city life can be so synthetic, and our work practices can be so clumsy, that we need banks of medical and remedial people on standby to fix us. Therapists, chiropractors, orthopaedics, eye doctors, herbalists... the list goes on. All these industries and millions more, thriving on the basis of a work-life paradigm that doesn't function as Nature intended it to. Most of what we learn about self-management is how to fix things, that should never be broken in the first place.

But relationships, families and self-worth are not so easy to fix. Once those things are broken we're facing some serious repair jobs, and most of that is really in vain. You can't repair lost time with children, or poor quality time with partners, once it's done it's done. Time itself is one of the most valuable and precious commodities in life. Once lost or given it can't be taken back, repaired or replaced. So, with family, relationships, productivity and self-worth, getting things right the first time might be a really sensational way to transform our work-life balance paradigm and save us a huge amount of time and energy. Not only that, it could save us a fortune in medical bills.

So, prevention is better than cure. And that requires wisdom. Wisdom comes with time, and time produces experiences which cause us to make mistakes that need cure. The aim here is to shortcut the process.

# Overcoming Distractions

So, "turning-up" is natural and easy when there are no distractions. I found this in my own career. When I first started speaking to audiences I'd prepare my talk one way, but deliver it totally different. Why? Because I "turned up" in practice when there was no audience to distract me, but when I was confronted by an audience the fear and desire to do good made me lose presence. I had to do a lot of work on myself to be natural in front of an audience.

When there are no distractions, like out in Nature, people "turn-up" automatically. People are really different in Nature. They are more creative, more generous, more present. When I take business groups into Nature, years drop off their face, and they start to get on well with each other, even if, back in the office they are rivals. Why? Because the ego is not in defence, distractions are less, the beauty is magnetic, people simply "turn-up" because there's no reason not to.

Now, this might come as a surprise but the best you, the most productive and energy efficient you that can do a day's work is the natural you. That person, is relaxed, happy, healthy and at ease. So, the real mission of work life improvement is to handle all those distractions that take you away from who you really are. In other words, without distractions - you "turn-up" in life automatically, and happily.

There are 3 different categories of distractions we need to deal with in order to be at our best. They are physical, mental and emotional.

Physical distractions range from pain and discomfort all the way through to hyperactivity caused by sugars, including food, alcohol and drugs. Mental distractions range from worry and stress all the way through to overwhelm and confusion. And emotional distractions range from sadness and grief all the way through to judgement and insecurity.

So, "turning up" is natural, and distractions are life. To stay authentic and natural, you'll need to deal with distractions. Even if you are playing Golf or making love, dealing with distractions is an important skill. How to block out mind noise? How to process emotion? How to prevent and deal with physical addictions?

# Prevent Physical Distractions

Physical distractions draw us away from "turning up" because it brings pain and discomfort into our awareness. When our body with it's habitual and insatiable appetite runs our life, there's just no way we can be present. Here are a few ideas to prevent that happening:

- Exercise daily.
- Eat fresh food.
- Stretch your body.
- Sit properly - good posture.
- Watch the energy of the moon.
- Get fresh air once a week.
- Minimise toxin consumption.
- Avoid excess acidity and alkalinity in food.
- Control your body - don't overdo things.
- Eat, sleep, drink and sex in moderation.
- Do moderation in moderation.
- Be thankful for your body.
- Watch your poop.
- Check your cholesterol.
- Get sunlight daily.
- Evolve your lungs.
- Expose yourself to pollutants gradually.
- Good bed.
- No wet hair or bare feet in the cold outdoors.
- Protect your kidneys from cold.
- Walk wherever you can, up steps instead of elevator, etc.
- Eat balanced diet. Not too much protein.
- Eat for your work life.
- Don't carry heavy -one sided shoulder bags.
- Learn how to relax actively.
- Measure your health by your immune system function.
- Don't medicate long term.
- Breathe right - Diaphragm should compress on exhale.
- Eat light at night.

## Prevent Mental Distractions

Mental distractions draw us away from "turning up" because they affect our capacity to communicate. These include Parkinson, Stroke, Alzheimer's, dilution, uncertainty and the most common, depression. Here're a few ideas to prevent that happening:

- Develop trust in a higher power.
- Have back up plans for your worst-case scenarios.
- Create buffer zones around fear - don't be run by them.
- Control your moods when you chose.
- Accept your incompetence as a part of life.
- Train your brain.
- Do creative arts as well as logical ones.
- Be intense - Focus on one job at a time.
- Look into people's eyes when you talk.
- Want nothing - have everything.
- Avoid numbness from alcohol - drugs.
- Learn to still your body with your mind.
- Measure your mind health by your nervous system.
- Practice recall daily - poems or numbers.
- Cool your mind by good views.
- Be in Nature.
- Prevent depression by eliminating righteousness.
- Create a personal vision.
- Create routines.
- Write it down - A short pencil is better than a long memory.
- Allocate priorities - set agendas - rigid schedules.
- Always be early.
- Avoid desperation.
- Do one task at a time within the time.
- Don't take on other people's stress.
- Fulfil your commitments.
- Do what you say.
- Listen to others intensively.
- Look for beauty everywhere.

# Prevent Emotional Distractions

Emotional distractions draw us away from "turning up" because they disempower us, make us reactive and unauthentic. We cannot remain in a state of presence while we have any emotion. So, emotional control is a vital element for anyone who chooses to "turn-up" in life. Here're a few ideas to prevent emotional distractions:

- Learn to observe your moods and feelings without reacting.
- Don't take yourself too seriously.
- Remove all ideas of blaming others for your emotional state.
- Be at peace in your heart every morning.
- Avoid upper and downer causing experiences.
- Accept both support and challenge as two sides of one coin.
- Remember infatuation leads to resentment.
- Mind doing what feels right - Most of the time is an emotion not intuition.
- Remember pleasure and pain come hand in hand.
- Learn to let go, expectations kill love.
- Know that all emotions are only half truths.
- Practice feeling things without acting on them.
- Remove - "Got to", "Ought to", "Should" from your vocabulary.
- Be thankful.
- Follow your heart.
- Don't react - first impressions are emotional ones.
- Have the wisdom of time. Seek the two sides of everything.
- Trust emotion to tell you how you feel - then change it.
- Choose your state of emotion, don't let it choose you.
- Be disciplined in your planning.
- Be in the moment in your lifestyle.
- Be soothed by water.
- Trust Nature.

# Emotions

The evolution of human consciousness reveals that we have capacities untapped in our ability to create, manage and do work, It reveals that we've been living in the stone age on mental application. So, we're going to step through the ways of "catching up" if you choose. The first, and fastest jump in human performance that you can invest in is the ability to actually, "turn-up" in whatever you do.

Doing anything by half is surely going to cost. It is going to cost double because both things that you've split your attention to are going to suffer. In an office, if our attention is distracted by phone calls, conversations, emails, people walking past, music, emotion, and our own personal distractions, we are not being productive. Who pays? Our family pays because we get home more tired, feeling less productive and late.

Turning up means that whatever is there, right in front of you is your highest priority no matter who it is. Call this focus, but it is not aggressive focus. You can attribute this single skill to the mastery of new Golf professionals, sports teams, actors and musicians. They are mastering the art of turning up. 100% in the zone whenever they choose.

If you have this skill, then, when you are talking to someone, or listening to someone, you are not scratching your bum or answering the mobile or dialling a text message. You are right there, 100% focussed and they'll feel it too. If you are in the taxi going to the airport, "turn up" with the taxi driver. If you are on the train, "turn up" with the sounds and experience. If you are home with your partner, you'll "turn up" with them.

It means that you need to become adept at handling emotion because emotions exist relative to the past or the future. Fear of the future and guilt about the past are the two primary emotions that drag us out of the moment and therefore cause us not to "turn-up."

"Turning up" is really easy once we know how. When we get away from all the stress, the worry, the ambition, the fear, the expectation - all the things we load onto our lives- we find ourselves, automatically, "turning-up" happy, vital, healthy and inspired with life.

# Emotional Fruitcake or Inspired Genius?

In order to "turn up" you'll need to know when and how to deal with emotion. It's your emotions that come most between you and your presence. So, if you know how and when to drop past those emotions back into your true Nature you can "turn up" whenever you choose.

How? By flipping this whole equation upside down and becoming aware of when you are not turning up. Your true Nature is already "turning-up" naturally, so the most vital skill in dealing with emotion is to be aware of it. You see, most people don't know the difference between emotion and inspiration.

Let me give you an example: Say you see something dramatic. An absolutely stunning sunset. There you are, in awe of it, just mesmerised. That's inspiration. Now, a friend is standing beside you and you turn and say, "Wow, look at that sunset." That's emotion.

So, getting into the zone of "no emotion" can take some time. Athletes prepare themselves, it's called psyching themselves up, and artists go into isolation for it. There are so many ways to get into the "no emotion" zone and as long as we know how, we're capable of sliding into that space. Again, the key is to know what it feels like. There are two critical measures; one is that you forget time, and the other is you forget space. In the zone, all that matters is what you are doing.

Being aware of when you are not in the zone is a vital skill for professional people at work too because when we're emotional at work we're likely to make a lot of foolish mistakes. That's where leadership is important because if you see people all emotional in the office, you know that their work is going to be substandard. Even clients know when their service drops, something is wrong.

So, next time you feel all emotional about someone at work or you are thinking about your annual holidays or last night's dinner, just say to your boss, "I know you are paying me, and because I haven't turned up, I mean really turned up fully, I am not able to do my job properly, so for this day, please don't pay me. I'm really not earning what you think I'm worth." I doubt this will catch on...

# Lower Emotion and Higher Emotion

There's a range of emotions, the lower of which is more destructive than the higher. So, if you plan to be emotional, try the higher ones at least.

Lower emotions are: anger, jealousy, resentment, sadness, grief, fear and guilt.

Higher emotions are kindness, compassion, gentleness and care.

Moving from lower to higher emotions requires gratitude. The more you can thank a person for, the higher the quality of emotion you are sharing with them. If you did a million thank yous you would end up in the zone, 100% in presence. That's like making love, you end up totally connected with your partner no matter what emotional state you started in.

So, we are trying to turn up at work and at home. In that state, we give people 100% attention, we listen, they feel met, and when we apply this to our own work, we hit the nail on the head every time.

Great artists and television presenters have to get into this zone quickly every single time they perform. Each has their own process but the area of the brain that they are tapping is the same for everyone. They tap their corpus callosum. This part of our brain can only think one thought, only transmit one signal. Here, we're totally tapping the higher consciousness of creativity and thought. We're inspired. Again, it's no big deal, it's natural and everyone can do it, if only they know the difference between an emotion and an inspiration.

Quickly tying this back to domestic bliss, if you turn up at home in emotion, then you could spend 12 months doing nothing more than pleasing your partner and they'd still complain. They'd still be missing you because you haven't really turned-up. Emotion means that either your body, your mind or your feelings are off somewhere else having a party, while you stand face to face with someone who wants your attention. They don't want 12 months attention, they want 5 minutes of absolute and total focus. Forget meditation, just learn to turn up for people and you'll be the enlightened master, or close at least.

# Getting In Touch

There are many layers to life. On the surface it's all pretty obvious. Under the surface it's a minefield of complexity.

The key to all this is, "don't give your power away."

There're gurus, and there're new age speakers, and there are healers, and there are mind readers, and astrologers, and there are spooky people who read your tea leaves. All these people are brilliant and have amazing power, but don't give your power away.

When your mind is turbulent it is easy to want someone else to straighten it out. And that's where the road gets bent out of shape. This is the time when you need to go bush, seek Nature's guidance, not listen to a guru.

I think there's an amazing untapped potential within all people and sure, it sometimes gets lost in the storm of emotions. But you need to hold fast to your own innerwealth, your strength.

People will tell you about past lives and future lives and cracks in your palm but they have a fragment of the story. You are the one who must tell your own future and that is within you.

The key is in your heart. Don't be afraid to use it. Understand that the only limit is set by the amount of noise you attract around you. Remember the emotions and judgements are the blocks.

So, if you want to know your destiny, clear out your unfinished emotional business, let go the judgements of yourself or others and go bush. Just walk the beach or sail a boat. Throw away the golf clubs, it spoils a good walk. Go and open yourself to Nature and you'll hear the most powerful guidance.

Bring that awareness to work and home and use the Laws of Nature to hold certainty. Don't ask advice from people you wouldn't pay. Don't listen to advice you didn't ask or pay for. The greatest advice you need to listen to is the advice you give others. Really, it is meant for you, not them.

# Tuning In

Our mind can play all sorts of tricks on us, and in many cases these tricks ruin our balance time. Take comparison for example. Here we are, standing on top of the second highest trekking peak in the world, looking at the summit of Mt Everest, watching the sunrise, and someone turns to me and says, "This so reminds me of France when I was there in 1834," or something like that.

Where are we when we compare things? Well, we are certainly standing on the spot right here, but our head is doing flips between what we're experiencing with our body and what we remember experiencing before. Now, our body doesn't know time. Memories of fears are as powerful as fears. So, when we are comparing where we are to some other experience, we're totally not "turning up."

So, say you go home to your partner after work and he or she wants time with you but you are comparing your day to the day you wished you had, or comparing your work to what you want to create. Where are you? Are you actually home sharing time with your partner or are you split, half "turning up."

I think 99% of relationship problems stem from this comparison thing. Our mind plays tricks on us. You can see that comparison might be fantastic when you're doing vision quest or setting goals. But when you are doing communication, if you are into comparison mode, then the other person, or people are just not going to pick up the signals you want them to get.

When we are doing comparison, it is like a radio that is not tuned into the station, actually it's receiving two stations at once. So, in fact you can't hear either one. So, you are not tuned into your own energy. This makes it impossible for people around you to pick up your message too.

It's very common. Most people talk about, "oh, when I was in..." or "when I get .... things will be better." This is comparison and it makes the whole potential of what we really want to say, dilute, especially if we are looking for quality time with family. If we're always comparing what's happening to what we want, we're not "turning-up."

# Intensity

"Turning Up" demands intensity. Sitting around watching TV is not turning up, actually, it's more like, "turning-off." So you can't value those activities as good mechanisms for balancing your life or even quality time with your family. Those are more like physical or mental rest periods.

Sometimes on a wintery weekend, my partner and I just sit and read books. It's a nice easy and restful. However, when Monday comes I often feel like the weekend escaped and I'm not really fresh for the start of Monday. What it really means is that I failed to be present over that weekend; I was in fairyland. Twenty hours of emotional companionship, or 40 hours of television is not going to balance your life. Those things in themselves are going to add the need for even more balance time. They'll compound your need for balance. On other winter weekends we go for brisk walks in the chill of the wind and share cuddles behind rock walls along the ocean coast. Monday comes and I feel like I've had a month's holiday.

It's the same in an office too. Many times, we take too long to do something because we don't have time pressure. Time pressure, that is a dead line that's fixed, forces creativity and intensity and so, the odds are that we'll be more present when we do that job and presence means quality.

So, it's a great mistake to think life is getting harder or that we're under more pressure now, than before. What it might be wise to consider is that we're being asked to be more intense, more present when we do things. This translates to doing more in less time.

Simply, it means that we're evolving toward a more effective lifestyle. If we meet someone, we're being asked to do it in less time, but with total presence. Or, of we are doing something at work, to do it once and do it well in a shorter period of time. In a sense it's taking the wasted time out of our life.

Intensity is not stressful. Intensity is only stressful if we're holding onto some outmoded idea of how we can work - live - play. Getting things done in less time is actually quite relaxing if you know how.

# Removing the Obstacles

Not all our work life balance is exactly how we "expect it" to be. So, to remain present with our everyday life we need to do some mental gymnastics. Learning mind games, or mental gymnastics, is a really important part of "turning up." Say something bad happens to us about 20 years ago, but we keep having drama around it. Then that event, and the person in it, is still running our life, 20 years later. Distracting our focus, draining our energy, sucking our life.

This affects our balance in life, because it makes it impossible to show up. We are always comparing, worried, protecting, projecting. We're stuck in the past, trying to act in the present, fearing the future. To expect any relationship to survive and thrive under those circumstances means we need someone of low self worth to tolerate it.

The best mental gymnastics, or mind games that I've found to work in bring people present in their day is the "balance game." Simply, this can help you cope with a family tragedy, a scar from the past or a fear of the future.

Here's how:

Take the event that is affecting you and split it into two lists. The first list is all the things that were bad about that event. The second list is all the things that were right about that event, the good news. Now, even a rape or violence teaches us something. So, really, in universal language, there're two sides to everything and the mission here in this first step is to find them. The two lists must end up the same length, equal balance of positive and negative. This kills the emotion from that event, but it's not finished.

Now, take all the things that went bad, and list all the good things that come from those. For example: someone might have broken your trust, the good thing is that you learned to value your intuition more. Then take all the good things that happen and find the downside of them. For example; if you started "self exploration," then the downside might be that you became hyper sensitive.

By the time you finish you'll be in the present. You'll let go the past.

# Be Present

People want to feel your presence before they talk to you, and if your presence is not genuine; all the talk in the world is not going to compensate for it. So, the art of good communication begins with silent communication.

All people are intuitive: they know when you are present and they know when you are emotional. So, much of human behaviour that can't be explained by psychological models is human Nature blocked by emotion.

Nearly 100% of child behaviour, and a huge amount of adult behaviour is spent trying to get attention from parents and work colleagues who can't "turn up." And it's taken very personally. People take our lack of presence as a sign that we don't like them, or we don't care. So, by turning up you save a lot of time.

You can come to peace within yourself and with the world by living from your true Nature in total presence, rather than in emotion. Being emotionally motivated is destructive because we're always trying to fix or change the world that actually doesn't need changing. So much of life is just how it is meant to be, and so much of our reactions are actually trying to fix what doesn't need to be fixed.

## Small Changes - Huge impact

Wanting to make radical and huge changes in your life is a presence killer too. So, resisting change altogether is a problem because it keeps you in the past but in the other extreme, too much ambition to change things, puts you into the future. People who are always ambitious and enthusiastic about the future, rarely show up in the moment.

Wanting the future makes us very accident prone, almost clumsy. We are distracted from the moment, keen to get somewhere better so, we start looking at where we want to be rather than refining where we are. This happens in relationships and business more than we care to mention.

In business, we can easily become obsessed with the future. The existing reality might be tough so we start visioning, imagining and trying to attract the right clients.

In relationship, we can also become obsessed with the future, it's like an anti depressant because the truth might be that our partner is not showing up, or we are into disappointment with them. So, if we come into our relationship wishing that our partner was different, or wishing that we had a different circumstance, we're no present at all, are we? We're not showing up.

When we aspire to change, we're typically in the belief set that something in the existing present moment is not good for us, or good for others. We don't know how to deal with it and so we create a future reality that's different. We reject the current situation and aspire for improvement. This can become a habit, a grave mistake, because we end up avoiding our abundance.

# Evolve not Change

The difference between evolving and changing is huge. A person who wants to change their business or personal circumstances is automatically rejecting their current position. There is an implied dissatisfaction. This is completely understandable, like in situations where there is abuse or turmoil. So, the desire for change is most likely based on rejection. There are two considerations here. Remembering that rejection is a powerful force, the witnessing and desire for change is highly motivating. So, this is the gift. The curse of change is that there is an automatic implication that "here" is not going to be as good as "there."

This is the wanting mind, and it really does become an overriding habit of life. It is the inability to relax into the current reality and therefore, creates a continuous tension of dissatisfaction.

When I first studied spirituality I came to it disillusioned with my life and therefore, dissatisfied with who I was and what I was doing. There were plenty of people ready to share my money and teach me how to be a better Chris. They accepted my paradigm, and in most cases reinforced it: Chris needed to change, they knew how it could be done and where I should end up.

In hindsight, which is always easy, what I really needed to do was evolve myself, rather than change it. The person who wants to evolve is accepting the current position as perfect but recognising the need for growth, is looking for more sophisticated ways of expressing it.

The key to evolution is that it is in a direction. So, again in retrospect, I would have been wiser at the start of my own spiritual journey, to have found a direction for my growth, rather than a generic, "gee, I want to be a better me." That direction did come for me eventually, and after 15 years of self-indulgent change work, I realised that there was nothing to change. All I really needed to do was to find the direction of my life, and refine my process for achieving it. I sat on a mountain top, wrote my life purpose, translated it into a vision, and since then, committed myself to better and better ways of moving toward it. Evolution is never random, it always moves in a direction, a purpose, an art. Goals are not the direction, just stepping stones along the way.

# Become Your Own Best Friend

Spending time, reconnecting with your roots, your heart and your soul, and balancing your emotions is a really vital part of work-life balance.

Do you sit down or lie down each day and say to yourself, "How are you today my friend? What do we need to evolve today? Is there any block to your love for life and what are we going to do about it?

I think it's great to become your own best friend. Give yourself whatever it takes in the form of self-diagnosis or get help with it. Your love for life, your job, and your partner is the single most important barometer of your process in life. If you can be your own best friend in this journey you'll arrive in your day, week, year totally authentic. And what more could you dream of. You might not be the world champion every day, but you can be your own best you.

I don't really know what a soul is, but I do know what it feels like when I connect to it. I used to sit in meditations and look at statues and things but, really for me, I was just emulating what others were doing. From a first hand perspective, I didn't come out of those experiences refreshed or in touch with my soul at all. I was in touch with my knees, my boredom, my aching back, but not my soul.

When I hug a tree or sit by a lake or paddle my kayak out in Sydney Harbour, I am in touch with my soul. No question about it. When I go to the mountains of Nepal and walk up those long hills, I am in touch with my soul. Totally. Even when I play my piano I get in touch with my soul, and I'm not very accomplished. The fact of the matter is, my soul and I are really good mates. We like each other.

To be your own best friend you've got to become the person you like to hang out with. In my experience it is important to learn how to be alone and be happy with it. To become your own best buddy and value that. This for me is one of the great keys to life. To learn that being alone is healthy, and the older we get, the healthier it is.

# Accept Rejection

What helped me most on my self-friendship journey was learning the Laws of Nature because they gave me a real expectation of who I could be. Once, I thought that I could be "good" and then it hurt when people accused me of doing something bad. I didn't like that, I took it very personally. However, I learned from Nature that the world is going to see me as both a good and a bad guy. Some people are going to like me, some people are going to reject me, no matter what I do.

It's the most amazing insight, because it just shows us that if we want to be our own best friend we have to accept that people are going to see the good side and the bad side of who we are. So, it's up to us to form our own opinion of who we are by holding integrity in our intentions.

No matter what you do, people are going to form an opinion of you. So, it's wiser to value how you feel about yourself rather than other people's opinion.

I recommend you do something each and every morning of your life to bring yourself back to balance. If you do this before you go out to work, you'll find it easier to stay in balance throughout the day. The real harmony is within. Please acknowledge that no one can treat you better than you treat yourself.

# Be Honest with Yourself

Sometimes we're doing well. Sometimes we're not. The important thing is to admit it. Not just to yourself, but admit it to others too.

People take your moods to heart. So, when there's a personal issue that gets between you and your self-respect, the best thing to do is admit it, own it and be a good friend, firstly to yourself and secondly to others.

Self-honesty is also important because it'll reveal how you feel about certain things that people do to you. When we're not self-aware it's easy to say, "it's ok, no problem," when really we mean, "you bastard, that hurt." Self-honesty is about knowing how you really feel about things. But it does not mean expressing them.

In the longer term I worked out the difference between owning my behaviour and expressing my reactions to people. You see, people do to us on the outside just what we're doing to ourselves on the inside. So, reacting to people is a waste of energy, they're just mirroring our own self-awareness. When we're a good friend to ourselves, so are others.

# Eat Great

To perform well at work, and in life in general, our bodies need the right fuel. Sugar, alcohol, packaged and reheated food, frozen food, dehydrated food, wheat, dairy foods and processed food with additives, affect our mind.

If you are really intent on clarity and open hearted living you'll need to be mindful of what food you eat and when.

Long delays between meals are bad, blood sugars affect your thought patterns. Sugars stimulate activity and make it hard to concentrate for long periods of time. Caffeine is addictive as a stimulant for thought.

There's a time and a place for everything so there's no right or wrong here. I'm simply pointing out that blurry thinking and mind control issues are 99% self induced and great thinkers eat well.

I'm no wowser - far from it. Even in Nepal I enjoy a few rice wines with Monks sometimes. Alcohol and stuff is a medicine in some circumstances. But if you're into it everyday, especially before breakfast, well, you're on the one-way train to old age fast. You'll probably fizzle before the grandkids get to know about you. So, for the sake of good health, know that the most destructive drug on earth is alcohol. So, cut it to once a week, and then a few glasses at best. You'll save 20 years on your life and, I can guarantee, your sex life will be much better.

# Beyond Self Obsession

The ultimate awareness in self-help is that there's no self to help. Our "self" in that model is our ego. And this ego is trans

ient. So, the more you learn to separate your emotions from your deeper soul, the less you consider that the "self" needs help.

In Nature, we eat to live. We don't fuss around too much with French sauce and herbal sprinklings. We have a day's work ahead and so, we eat for that. We treat our body with respect, and rather than focus on inches or pounds, we're concerned with doing what we are called to do, every day. So, we eat to live. If we're lazy we eat less if we're chopping wood for the fire, we eat more. It's a matter of choosing our diet for function rather than for pleasure.

Back in the city, when we scan the menu we're thinking about taste. We think about food as a source of pleasure. This is our wanting mind again. Always wanting more or better. Never happy for long and it reveals the folly of trying to do any form of self-help in order to cause us to be content. In the wanting mind, there's just never enough.

Becoming content with yourself, is a huge part of life balance. Contentment is a natural state of mind but it is a foreign state of mind in a consumer world where the ego is the basis for choice. If you can learn contentment you'll be more happy, more inspired and more at peace. But it means really understanding your Innerwealth and the difference between this and your ego.

Contentment means happy with what you've got. Frankly, we're afraid of it. We're afraid of contentment because in that comfort and stillness we don't want anything. What then? If we're perfectly happy with what we've got, then who and what is going to motivate us? This is a very important question and only the individual who gets to contentment will truly know the answer. All the rest is theory.

## Balance one - Forget the other

The best way to understand the idea of personal balance is to consider that there are two of you. Two people. One of them is Mr. or Mrs. Happy; totally content, completely worriless. This person has four simple principles for life. Kindness, gentleness, care and love. They come automatically with a connection to Nature.

Now, there is the other you. This is your "always wanting" self, you can call it, Mr. or Mrs. Wanting. This you, your ego and emotion, always wants more. This "wanting you" is really important because it wants wealth in order to make a home, or it wants better health in order to stay young, or it wants a better relationship in order to enjoy the home life so it keeps you hungry, exploring and challenged by life. Remember the first you is content.

Both co-exist, but one of these two has to take priority in your life. Mr. or Mrs. Wanting can never achieve sustained happiness. Mr. or Mrs. Happy can never create desires, drama and goals. The key is not to get them confused.

So, no matter how much balance time or energy you spend trying to satisfy your wanting mind, it will never be happy or content for long. And no matter how much work you do, your contented mind is never unhappy.

When you focus on your innerwealth, your contentment, a certain shine comes to your eyes, a glow to your demeanour. Again, it is perfectly natural out in Nature but it takes a bit of work to stay in touch with it in city life.

That's why I think meditation or yoga or some other sort of self mastery physical and mental practice is a really important training ground for your city life. I don't think those things are really necessary if you live in Nature, but in the city, they are really helpful.

And keeping your feet firmly connected to the earth, the Laws of Nature make your contentment transportable. With those laws you can go anywhere in the city and still be connected to Nature.

# Independence is Vital

Nothing of the senses ever satisfies the Soul. Things don't make you happy. Eventually we all die, and every-thing that we had is gone. Nothing is permanent so, learn to hold your emotional wellbeing independent of things.

No matter how much we collect, own, consume or experience, our soul, is never satisfied by the accumulation of things. That's why consumerism fails, no matter how good products get, people are never content, so, the marketing machine just builds a new mouse trap. It's a self-perpetuating process. It feeds itself.

Moments of real contentment - inspired moments - linger in your memory for your entire life. Moments when you were so overwhelmed by love and happiness, there was no wanting, nothing to change, perfect moments in life.

The real desire for balance is the desire for these moments. The wanting mind at work comes home and wants these moments. We have to allow ourselves to become independent of material life just a few hours a day at least, so that we connect to our soul, and the soul of those we love. When we are in our true Nature, we are really connected to everything, and everyone.

The skill of balance, to a large extent, is the skill of contentment. Accessing Mr. or Mrs. Happy. This mindset only appears when we are thankful for what we have. Even the most devastating circumstance has a good and a bad side. The wanting mind can't see it, because it is an emotional mind, only seeing half the story.

Cultivate this idea of two minds. Cultivate the idea that one part of you can be in perfect peace while the other part might be experiencing a hurricane. Imagine a tree in a huge storm. Its leaves and branches being ripped from its core, but deep down under the soil, its roots, like your soul, is solid, unaffected: independent.

# Balance the Hour - Get a life

Work can suck time. If you give your work an open checkbook of time, it'll take it. For some people this is a great escape from relationships and health commitments, but for most of us, balance is necessary. So, the important thing here is remaining vigilant on our time commitments. Time isn't everything but it sure means a lot.

A lot of people stuff around at work, because they really deeply don't want to go home. Don't hide behind work. Plan your day, plan it well and plan the time allocations for all the aspects of life. Don't wait to be sick to get healthy. Don't wait until your partner leaves you to get home on time. Don't wait for opportunities to leave you in order to make a change in your life. Get the most out of life now that you have the opportunity, don't wait until it is too late.

Stress is cumulative. Yesterday's unfinished business rolls over to today. And today's to tomorrow. So, balance needs to be considered as a progressive process. However, current work-life balance techniques are quite chunky, for example: work all day, seek balance at night after work. So, in this old model people are stressed all day and want balance afterward. This is why alcohol and food have become so abused. People trying to balance one controlled situation with another out of control.

I think it's more rational and healthy to bring balance into every hour of the day, rather than into 5-day working chunks with 2-day weekend breaks. I subscribe to the idea of work time and home time, that's not the argument here. I am talking about the quality of the time spent during those five working days.

The main thing I do, throughout my working day, is to maintain my contentment. I hold my state of mind in contentment whenever I can. Even if the work I am doing is not "great" or "joyful" I hold my state of mind as the most precious independence I can have, happiness, and this is ultimatly 24/7 balance.

# The Greatest Human Power

I know that my happiness is totally in my control, right here and now. I can change my perspective and see balance in any situation and therefore change my mind about it. Now, instead of fixating on things being right or wrong, I look for the gift, the benefit in that situation. I remain happy, and therefore I usually get to act authentically.

For me, it's like keeping my feet firmly planted on the earth, in the spirit of happiness at all times. And from that great place, not wanting to change anything or anyone, grounded in gratitude, I do my life work. I set my goals from a place of not wanting.

At first I found transitioning backward and forward between my wanting mind and my contentment a little lumpy. Learning how to be mindful of this was a really interesting journey because I kept wanting when I was meant to be content. Like I'd go into Nature to do a walk and find myself saying, "I'll be happier when I get to the top of this hill." Those old habits are hard to get past.

Please don't get me wrong, I still get out of balance. I'm still emotional and I still get angry with myself. I still get confused and have moments where I am not content. Goodness, that's not what I'm going to pretend. I still have those moments of reaction, but instead of acting on them, I simply see myself as an evolving being. I am content, with my discontent.

One day, after weeks of meditation in a retreat I found myself permanently content. There was nothing in that environment to disturb my mind. I was at peace. At the end of the program I went to the teacher and expressed my pride in my achievement. He quickly responded, "now your problem is you will be discontent if you are not content. You've made your world smaller, not bigger."

A Peaceful mind is a mind that finds the process of being in peace, rather than an environment in which it is peaceful. Once, after weeks in Zen, I caught a taxi to the airport. We were late, I began to sweat. 3 weeks of peace, vaporised in an hour. The greatest human power is the process of adapting to circumstance and holding that inner peace.

www.ingramcontent.com/pod-product-compliance
Ingram Content Group UK Ltd.
Pitfield, Milton Keynes, MK11 3LW, UK
UKHW020118200726
13856UKWH00002B/610